P9-BYD-350

MAN to MAN

Helping Fathers Relate to Sons
and Sons Relate to Fathers

Dr. Earl R. Henslin

Henslin Communications
Brea, California

MAN TO MAN
Helping Fathers Relate to Sons
and Sons Relate to Fathers
Copyright © 1993, 2001 by Dr. Earl R. Henslin
Published by *Henslin Communications*

International Standard Book Number 1-929753-04-7

Written by Earl R. Henslin, Psy.D.
Edited by Chelese Guthrie Palmer
Proofread by Denise Dulberg, Pamela Inman
Cover & Book Designed by Charles Schnur

Printed in the United States of America

ALL RIGHTS RESERVED
No part of this publication may be reproduced, stored in a retrieval system, or transmitted in any form or by any means—electronic, mechanical, photocopying, recording, or otherwise—without prior written permission, except for brief quotations in critical reviews or articles.

Scripture quotations are taken from the HOLY BIBLE, NEW INTERNATIONAL VERSION®, NIV®. Copyright © 1973, 1978, 1984 by International Bible Society. Used by permission of Zondervan Publishing House. All rights reserved.

The Twelve Steps are reprinted with permission of Alcoholics Anonymous World Services, Inc. Permission to reprint and adapt the Twelve Steps does not mean that AA has reviewed or approved the contents of this publication, nor that AA agrees with the views expressed herein. AA is a program of recovery for alcoholism only—use of the Twelve Steps in connection with programs which are patterned after AA, but which address other problems, does not imply otherwise.

The names of persons and certain details of case histories described in this book have been changed to protect the author's clients. In certain cases, composite case histories have been constructed from actual cases.

NOTE: This book is designed to provide information on the subject matter covered. It is provided with the understanding that the publisher and author are not engaged in rendering individualized professional services. These processes and questions are intended for group or individual study, and are not designed to be a substitute for one-to-one professional therapy when such help is necessary.

For information:
Henslin Communications
745 S. Brea Blvd., Ste. 23
Brea, CA 92821
Phone (714) 256-2807   Fax (714) 256-0937
www.DrHenslin.com

The book of Proverbs promises many good things to the son who heeds his father's wisdom and obeys his father's instructions. The father-son relationship is the most defining relationship in a boy's life. Yet it is one of the most neglected and misunderstood in our world today.

In his book *Man to Man,* Dr. Earl R. Henslin reminds fathers of the awesome responsibility we have in the nurturing of our sons. He helps men face the wounds that sons bear because of the father's failure and neglect. He shows us the impact this wound has upon a man's life, in his family, and on our society. And he offers us biblical principles for forgiveness, healing, and hope.

Men need one another. Sons need a connection to their fathers. Not just for discipline, provision, or guidance. Our sons need an emotional and spiritual bond in which they share their father's heart and soul. But that's not always possible with a father and son. Still, the need can be met. Other men can step in and be there for that boy. They can be there throughout a man's life. That's the benefit and joy of the Body of Christ. We are family willing to share burdens and care for one another.

Dr. Henslin teaches us how to build bridges of healing between fathers and sons, and man to man. Friendship between men is not easy. Fellowship in church is even tougher. But in these pages I found help for any man who is willing to seek growth.

God used this book in my life. It opened a door in my heart for God to work his wonderful grace. After reading *Man to Man*, I called Dr. Henslin and asked him to send a copy to my son Andy.

Being father to my children is one of the most important and sacred jobs God gave me. I learned along the way that children spell love: T-I-M-E. That time is precious, and all too short. The wise father will listen to his children, communicate his unconditional acceptance, impart his values, and model his faith in God.

Listen, we don't need more coaches to motivate our kids, we need more fathers to love them. We don't need men who are challenged, we need men who are changed! God will use this book to change men's hearts. Willing fathers will be helped, and wounded sons will be healed.

Charles Stanley

PUBLISHER'S PREFACE
for the Revised Edition

The revised edition of *Man to Man* has a number of significant improvements. The entire text of the book was revised to improve the readability of the material. The author, Dr. Earl R. Henslin, wanted the book to be accessible to more readers.

At the end of each chapter, Dr. Henslin has added a section titled *A Closer Look*. It is an opportunity for readers to focus on the key ideas and principles developed in the chapter. At the chapter's end there is also an opportunity for *Personal Reflection*. Dr. Henslin has provided questions that will help readers apply the material to their lives.

In the revised editon, Dr. Henslin has added an appendix to provide more information and resources for readers who would like to further pursue this topic or expand their journey toward recovery. The appendix begins with *A Word on Brain Chemistry*. This insightful addition helps readers understand that some problems exist because of inbalances within the neurobiology of a person's brain. Therapy and counseling may prove ineffective for some until they receive appropriate medical treatment.

Suggestions for Group Study and Support provides practical insight about organizing and conducting a small group meeting. Dr. Henslin answers some common questions and concerns about a small group. He has provided a *Suggested Meeting Format*, and added an important section titled *Guidelines for Sharing* to keep the meetings safe and nurturing.

An appendix for *Recovery Resources* is also included. It lists a number of organizations and groups that provide twelve-step recovery support for a number of problems. A *Suggested Reading List* offers written resources and recommended reading for specific needs.

May these pages provide you a pathway toward healing or improving your own father-son relationships. May you begin a new journey toward recovery, wholeness, and hope. And may you understand that your healing journey is never a solitary road. Your constant companion is also your Creator—the perfect Father.

The Publisher

DEDICATION

For Ben:

I respect and admire the man you are becoming. I am sorry where I have failed you, and I pray that you may find a community of deeply feeling and spiritually committed Christian men to support and be with you on your journey through life. May God richly bless and guide you as you grow in your relationship with the heavenly Father and in relationship with men here on earth. May he richly bless you as you develop the great gifts and abilities he has given you.

I love you,
Dad

CONTENTS

CHAPTER 1

The Wound
All Men Bear

There's a saying in the South: "No man is a man until his father tells him he is." It means that someday when you're 30 or 40, grown up, this man—whom you respect and love and want to love you—puts his arms around you and says, "You know, you're a man now, and you don't have to do crazy things and get into fist fights and all that to defend the honor of men. You don't have to prove anything. You're a man, and I love you."[1]

Actor Burt Reynolds opened his heart in this interview and revealed more about his relationship with his father:

> We never hugged, we never kissed, we never said, "I love you." No, we never cried.
> So what happened was that I was desperately looking for someone who'd say, "You're grown up, and I approve of and love you, and you don't have to do these things anymore." I was lost inside. I couldn't connect. I was incomplete. I didn't know then what I needed to know.[2]

Reynolds expressed the feelings of separation and woundedness that most men suffer in relationship with their fathers. Most men, no matter what age, hunger for approval and love from other men. They hunger for a strong emotional bond with their fathers. Without that bond and love and approval, they are wounded—torn at the heart.

This father-son wound causes men to do crazy things. Many men deny their physical pain. They may refuse to see a doctor for the injury to their backs or the sharp pain in their chests. Many men take foolish risks or participate in daring pastimes. They may race motorcycles, skydive, bungee-jump off bridges, or snowboard or ski in unmarked slopes. Many men live life close to the edge. They may work themselves to death. They push beyond fatigue, ignore exhaustion, rely on adrenaline, and abuse their bodies.

Men compensate for their inner wound, but they damage themselves and those around them. Our society and its families suffer desperate problems as men seek to address the wound in their relationships with their fathers. The father-son wound is the root that brings forth a man's most troubling issues. The key to a man's masculine maturity lies first in his relationship with his father and second in his relationships with other men.

The All-Important Relationship

God created a fundamental need within all boys (and girls too) to have an emotional connection with their fathers. Beginning with Adam and Eve, scripture records the importance of family. The father-son relationship had great meaning and importance to God. He identified himself as the God of Abraham, Isaac, and Jacob— three generations of fathers.

The important father-son connection is found throughout the Bible. Jacob lied, manipulated, and deceived to gain his father's blessing (Genesis 27:1- 29). God cautioned Eli about his weak and broken relationship with his two sons. God warned Eli that his failure would bring serious consequences (1 Samuel 2:22-36). Absalom, David's exiled son, faced death rather than live with his father's rejection (2 Samuel 14:28-33). Solomon praised his father's instruction throughout the book of Proverbs (Proverbs 4:1-4).

A boy's developing personality needs a relationship with his father. A boy needs an emotional and physical connection. An infant boy needs to feel his father's strong arms. This gives him physical security and emotional warmth. A toddler needs his father's empathy and quick response to bumps and bruises. This fosters a sense of comfort and safety. A boy needs his father's encouragement to take risks and ride a bike. This nurtures learning and courage. A boy needs his father's presence when he falls off that bike. This instills trust and the confidence to try again.

An adolescent boy needs a father who deeply loves the boy's mother. This models the character of a husband. A boy needs a father who has an intimate relationship with God. This demonstrates the spiritual reality from within the father's heart. A young man needs a father who offers emotion and physical support without demanding anything in return. This frees the son to pursue his own direction and become the man God desires. And when a boy becomes a man, he needs a father who accepts him, loves him, and relates to him as a man.

Every boy needs a father. A God-given space for a father awaits filling. A mother can never fill the void. She can only meet the need a boy has for a mother. The father-son relationship is God's intended source for these needs. This man-to-man connection builds the foundation on which a boy develops and matures into manhood.

The father is the one who models what it means to feel and express emotions. He models spiritual maturity and leadership. He models how to survive and provide for a family. He models values like integrity, purity, compassion, and obedience to God.

God never intended fathers to do this job alone. He works through families and through the community of God's people. The father-son relationship is the foundation and starting point. For a boy to develop his full masculine potential, he needs the input of a variety of other men. The making of a man takes a lifetime and a company of men throughout that lifetime.

The Father-Son Relationship Is Flawed

The father-son relationship is the most significant relationship in a man's life. But it is not perfect. There are no perfect fathers and no perfect sons. Fathers make mistakes—sons suffer wounds. The important families noted in the Bible bear these father-son wounds. Adam had the first two sons, still one murdered the other. Abraham fathered Ishmael with Hagar, and then sent them away.

Isaac blessed Jacob and thus wounded Esau. Jacob showed love for his son Joseph, yet his beautiful gift stirred jealousy among his other sons. King David's sons, Amnon and Absalom, were wounded in heart—neither healed. The father of the prodigal loved both his sons, yet each suffered in their relationship with him.

Few fathers would intentionally wound their sons. Most fathers do their best to care for their families and love their sons. They work hard to provide for their families. They deserve honor and respect for their personal sacrifices. But many fathers believe that material provision communicates love. It does not—it demonstrates responsibility. Love requires physical and emotion expression. Sons are thankful for fathers who provide, but they yearn for fathers who express affection.

Most fathers have no idea that they need to provide for spiritual and emotional needs in addition to the material ones. An emotional and spiritual bond with their sons is difficult. They experienced no such bond with their own fathers. Despite the fathers' best intentions and heartfelt motives, their sons are wounded and do not feel their love.

I lead workshops with men across the country. Many men in their 70s and 80s express lasting grief about their relationships with their fathers. They lived their lives without knowing if their fathers truly loved or cared about them. Most men today, whatever their age, suffer the same wound. They limp along with no sure knowledge of their fathers' love.

When a Son Doesn't Feel Loved

A son cannot feel secure in his father's love unless his father expresses love through words and actions. A father may think that the gift of a car says "I love you." A father may think he expresses love when he bails his son out of trouble. Or a father may think that financial help means love. But none of these sincere expressions can make a son feel loved.

Consider the story of IBM founder Tom Watson and his son Tom Watson, Jr. In his book *Father, Son, and Co.*, Tom Watson, Jr. chronicles the rise of IBM. From a company that made time-clock punch cards, IBM became a world leader in computer development. But Tom Jr. also tells another story. He describes a son who hungered to hear his father say, "I love you. You're doing a great job."

Tom Watson, Jr. grew up with every social, financial, and educational advantage. His father was a role model of integrity, honesty, and charity. He was fiercely loyal to his wife and children. He employed a male secretary to remove the potential for or accusation of unfaithfulness to his wife. Still, Tom Jr. had to share his father with the demands of an influential company with explosive growth. His father traveled the country to market products and to meet people of influence and power. His father scrambled to generate business in periods of decline. He worked hard to avoid employee layoffs. There are not enough hours in the day for a man to build an empire like IBM and be available for his kids. So the connection that suffered was between father and son.

As a young man, Tom Jr. was a playboy and spoiled rich kid. World War II gave wings to his love of flying—something his father hated. He became a pilot in the U.S. Army and was an aide and pilot for General Bradley. Tom's hard-driving, demanding ways cost him the rapport and respect of his flight crew. This changed young Tom Jr. from a spoiled, egocentric, rich kid into a leader. He began to affirm his men and respond to their emotional needs. They, in turn, became loyal and supportive to him. Far away from his father, Tom Jr. discovered what it took to be a leader.

Tom struggled with his postwar plans. He could stay in the service, or work with his father and one day lead IBM. Tom discussed his concerns with General Bradley. He wondered if he had the ability to follow in his father's footsteps. The general was confident that Tom could do the job, and he said that he could not imagine Tom doing anything else. This was the assurance Tom needed to go back home and work with his father.

As I read the story, I could almost hear the voice of the little boy inside Tom Jr. crying out for the love, approval, and acceptance of his father. He needed to know that the man he respected and admired above all others truly believed in him. Every son needs to feel this kind of love from his father. Every man needs to feel this kind of love deep within his soul.

A father communicates love by an emotional connection with

his son. He forges a bond with his son through concern about his child's feelings. He forges a bond through a simple hug to chase away tears. He forges an emotional bond through heartfelt recognition—even if it's praise for the scribbles of his three-year-old boy. He forges a bond by the value he places on his son's complaint of a playground injustice. And he forges a bond by participation in his son's experiences and activities. Without this emotional bond between father and son, a son will feel lost and unloved. And a disconnected son will do the crazy things Burt Reynolds mentioned.

Discovering the Wound

Most men never realize that they have suffered a wound in their relationship with their fathers. Or they discover this father-son wound later in life. Men in their early 20s have so much drive for sports or women or work that they are unaware of deep-seated feelings. Men remain unaware of their feelings because they are not expected to deal with them. Their feelings are not valued, probed, or challenged by other men. So they get away with ignoring their pain and confusion.

Most men will not deal with their woundedness until they are forced to. Often a life-shattering event triggers deep unresolved wounds: alcohol or drug abuse, emotional chaos at home, crazed kids, the threat of divorce, physical disability, career loss, etc. I didn't realize that something was amiss in my life until I reached my 30s. Over time I became aware of my own father-son wound.

Things began to change when I met Bill Henslin, a distant cousin. I met Bill after my move from Minnesota to Southern California. My great-uncle in Minnesota—also named Bill Henslin— told me to look him up. He said that I'd probably like him. Until that moment, I didn't know I had any relatives in Southern California. After I got settled, I followed up on my uncle's suggestion.

I parked in front of Bill's house and walked up to the door. My mouth was dry and my hands were cold and clammy. The excitement had me on edge. I didn't know what to expect. I was about to meet, face-to-face, a distant relative, the son of one of my great-grandfather's brothers. This man had actually known my great-grandfather, Frank Henslin, who was born in 1852 (100 years before my birth). Bill was my link to previous generations. He could tell me some of the legacies of my family.

Before I was halfway to the house, the door opened. An older man stepped out and walked briskly toward me. The moment was both warm and wonderful. Here was an older man who looked forward to meeting me! He was straight and tall with a distinguished presence and good looks. His broad smile radiated a life and energy rarely seen in the men of my family. I was struck by the resemblance to my grandfather, who died when I was 18. He also resembled my great-uncle, who had always been kind to me.

He approached with his hand extended. Then with my hand in his, he searched my eyes and declared, "I can tell you are a Henslin. You must be a fine young man. I'm happy to meet you." He was a mixture of warmth, gentleness, and sincerity. I could feel his pleasure and joy in our meeting.

It may seem like an ordinary greeting. But to me it was a new experience. This man assumed the best about me from our first encounter. In those first moments, I felt more positive affirmation and genuine expression of caring and warmth than I had ever felt from most of the other men in my family.

I felt an "I love you" from Bill Henslin's greeting, and I felt it with a depth that I had never experienced before. Our meeting awakened an awareness within me. I felt a deep sadness and grief inside. My relationship with Bill gave birth to the realization: *I had missed out on something significant in my relationship with my father. And I have also missed this in my relationships with other men in my family.*

A few years later I heard Robert Bly speak. Bly is a poet and storyteller. He used to travel the country and speak about men, masculine needs, and the father-son wound. The observations he shared about men opened my eyes. Bly's words uncovered the depth of sadness and grief within me. My emptiness—my wound—was the result of my relationship with my father. This was a wound I had not only received from my father, but also shared with him. I am sure my grandfather also bore that wound. This father-son pain had been passed on by men in my family for generations, perhaps centuries.

The men in my family are hard-working, good men. Still, most of them are disconnected from their feelings. That is the norm for upper Midwestern farm families like ours. We value hard work and we bear whatever physical or emotional pain comes our way. It is considered noble to suffer in stoic silence. *Men do not feel—* that is our unspoken rule. For that reason, men in our family know little about emotional expression. Hearty laughter, a warm hug from strong arms, or a spontaneous "I love you" are rare from the men in my family.

The lack of emotional connection between father and son is a tragic loss. These fathers love their sons. I know my father loved me. I know he cared. He worked hard, sacrificed for his family, and was a good provider. Still, he did not know how to help me feel loved. I know my father did not feel loved by his father. He received no affirmation from his father. I doubt that he ever felt the warm comfort of a hug from his father. So, my father could not give what he had not received. He could not reach out to me with tender emotions. No one had ever reached out to him.

Most men have suffered the same wound as the men in my family. They have never known an emotional connection to their fathers. They don't know how it feels. And they don't known how their fathers feel about them. Fathers may feel that their sons are diligent students, good athletes, successful businessmen, or fine family men. But without expression, those feelings—pride, admiration, respect—are locked inside the fathers' hearts.

The Emptiness Within

Most fathers have good feelings about their sons. Most fathers respect their sons and are proud of their accomplishments. They just don't know how to share those feelings. So most men, as Burt Reynolds described, feel lost, disconnected, and incomplete. A deep sadness exists in place of their fathers' affirmation and affection.

Today, more and more men experience the emptiness of a lost father-son connection. Many more sons have less and less time with their fathers. And in many cases, the limited time sons have with fathers is not "quality time." Robert Bly states, "The average father in the United States talks to his son less than 10 minutes a day. And that talk may be talk from a distance, such as 'Is your room cleaned up?' or 'Are you on drugs?'"[4]

In agricultural times, sons experienced work with their fathers side by side. Direct expressions of love may have been rare. Still, they had the opportunity to be with their fathers for many hours a day. Maturing boys, over the past six or seven decades, rarely have such intimate, daily contact with their fathers.

Today, many fathers work in offices or factories. They may spend long hours commuting to work and home. Others have jobs that require traveling Monday through Friday. They struggle to fit the week's yard work, family time, and household responsibilities into a weekend. Some work in other parts of the world for weeks or months at a time. Phone calls, e-mails, and packages replace personal contact. Still, other fathers must work more than one job to make ends meet. Under such circumstances, it is difficult for a father to have an intimate, emotional relationship with his son. Yet the son's need for an emotional bond with his father remains the same. The lack of the father-son relationship creates a devastating wound.

The emotional loss that a man experiences moves him to do two things. He seeks to prove himself to his father. And he tries to fill the emptiness in his soul. This emotional drive is often the dominant force that moves him. It leads to dysfunction and threatens every aspect of his life.

Proving One's Worth to Dad

Every boy yearns to be sought out by his father. When a boy lacks this emotional connection, he tries to cause his father to demonstrate his love for him. The boy tries to do something to create an emotional bond between them. Different boys try different behaviors. One boy may be an overachiever. He thinks, *If I do well in school or sports, Dad will think I'm special.* Another boy may cause trouble at home or school to gain his father's attention. Regardless of behavior, the motivation is the same—to be emotionally connected or close to father.

I excelled in music and sports when I was young. In ninth grade, I played first trumpet in the senior band. By tenth grade, I played on the varsity basketball team. Every time I did well, I waited for that big hug from Dad. I waited for him to tell me that I did good. But the hug and the words never came.

I grew older and more depressed. Smiles were rare. I spent a lot of time alone. Isolation was easier. I could hide the hurt. Still, I wanted my father to recognize my pain. I wanted him to reach out to me. I needed an emotional connection from him to ease my discomfort. But my father was unable to respond, and his inability fueled my depression.

Every boy believes he can do something to make that emotional connection with his father. He believes that if he does the right thing, his father will approve of him. He believes he can earn his father's affection. But that's not true. The father, not the son, is the one who must build the emotional bridge between them. Still, the myth persists. Inside many adult men there is a little boy trying to prove himself to his dad.

For example, Tom Watson, Jr. struggled well into adulthood, to earn his father's approval. But no amount of performance can produce the emotional bond a son seeks. That connection begins when the father reaches out to his son. Many boys will never experience that connection. These boys must wait for adulthood to begin the process of healing. As adults, they may also attempt to make an emotional connection with their fathers (see Chapter 8).

Filling the Emptiness Inside

A man will do almost anything to fill the ache and emptiness of the father-son wound. Some men resort to angry and destructive behaviors. Some bury their pain in a variety of addictions: work, alcohol, sex, food, or drugs. Some men immerse themselves in religious activity. They serve on church boards and committees, but rarely touch people's hearts. Some men put all of their feeling and passion into their yards or homes. They accomplish great home improvement projects, but neglect the family. They maintain a meticulous yard, but overlook the nurture of their children.

Fortunate men try positive ways to fill the emptiness inside. Significant relationships with other men is helpful. For example, after I met Bill Henslin and embraced my sense of loss and grief, I realized that I had been seeking out substitute fathers for years. In my late teens, I discovered value in my relationships with men. I searched for male friends who could meet my needs and comfort my hurts. The little boy inside me was in touch with this need. The child within me, who had suffered the father-son wound, encouraged me to grow in a world of men. I realized that a trustworthy man was a valuable and precious gift.

I had begun to heal my father-son wound. I discovered deep relationships with other men in the absence of an emotional bridge with my father. It was the next best thing. I was fortunate to have discovered the same thing David found in his relationship with Jonathan. When David mourned the death of his friend Jonathan, he said: "I grieve for you, Jonathan my brother; you were very dear to me. Your love for me was wonderful, more wonderful than that of women" (2 Samuel 1:26).

In my writing I use a number of terms that may be unfamiliar to some readers. I also put my own spin on some common terms. In this revision edition, I have added a section titled *A Closer Look* at the end of each chapter. It is not a glossary, but an aid to help readers understand and focus on key principles developed in the book. *A Closer Look* contains terms, concepts, and ideas that I want no one to miss.

The strength of my personal experience comes from three important influences in my life. Like a strong rope with intertwined cords, three significant elements combine in my life. The first of those three cords is my personal, Christian faith and my confidence in the Bible as God's standard for life. The second is my professional education and clinical experience as a counselor. The third cord is my own personal recovery journey with the Twelve Steps, which includes the support I have found within the recovery community.

The combination of these influences affects my use of language and my understanding of the terms chosen for *A Closer Look*. But more importantly, these three influences enrich my life and increase my ability to help others.

A Closer Look

The Father-Son Connection *(or "Bridge" or "Bond")*—An emotional and spiritual connection between a father and his son is a bond of feelings, values, and truth. A connected father is emotionally available to his son. He is in touch with his own feelings, and open and responsive to his son's. A connected father can express the affection he feels and the value he places on his son. He can stay in touch with reality about himself and his child.

This connection also offers an unfailing "God on earth" type of spiritual assurance and security during the best and worst of times. The sure connection and presence of the earthly father teaches the sure presence and availability of the heavenly Father. It establishes a platform of security from which a son can venture into new territory and take risks.

The father-son connection is also the key to a man's masculine maturity. A boy's growth into manhood lies first in his relationship with his father and second in his relationships with other men.

The Father-Son Wound—Sons are wounded when the important bond between father and son is weak or nonexistent. A father's absence, abandonment, or abuse are often to blame. Men can carry that wound throughout life.

This father-son wound causes men to do crazy things to compensate for their inner need. The father-son wound is the root that brings forth a man's most troubling issues.

Heart—When I use the word *heart*, I am referring to an emotional and spiritual place within each person. It is the seat of a person's emotions, affections, and personal reality—their true self. It is where we are honest with ourselves—our heart of hearts. People often say, "In my heart, I know that...." What they mean is that in that truest place within themselves—where personal honesty and certainty exists—they know their own personal reality about what they feel, what they value, and what they believe is true.

The first two usages of the word *heart* in the Bible are quite interesting to me. They appear in the book of Genesis chapter six just before the great flood. And they are used together—just one verse apart. Verse 5: *"The LORD saw how great man's wickedness on the earth had become, and that every inclination of the thoughts of his heart was only evil all the time."* Verse 6: *"The LORD was grieved that he had made man on the earth, and his heart was filled with pain."* Scripture refers to the same place (the heart) within man and within God. But each was filled with a different content. Man's heart was filled with evil—evil emotions, evil affections, and evil or corrupt reality. God's heart was filled with pain—painful emotions about the state of man, painful affections about God's relationship to man, and painful reality about what must happen to man.

I write about a father-son connection that builds a bridge between two hearts. It is a connection and disclosure of emotions, affections, and reality—truth. It is a father who expresses his feelings, reveals his values, and speaks his truth. But what if the father or another person's heart is filled with evil, deception, wicked affections, misplaced values, cruel emotions? For this, scripture warns: *"Above all else, guard your heart, for it is the wellspring of life"* (Proverbs 4:23). And how do we guard our hearts? Boundaries.

One more important reason to understand and guard the heart is *hope.* Hope enters through the heart. The heart is hope's door. The Apostle Paul prayed for the folks he had nurtured in faith. Among his prayer requests for the Ephesian church was this function of the heart. He said, *"I pray also that the eyes of your heart may be enlightened in order that you may know the hope to which he has called you..."* (Ephesians 1:18). So when a father nurtures his son's heart through an emotional and spiritual connection, he enables him to see and grasp hope. When a son's heart is unattended or wounded, he is kept from hope's light. His heart can easily grow dark—hopeless.

Soul—In the chapter, I refer to the soul as a place where a son can experience profound injury from the father-wound. The soul is often described as a person's mind, will, and emotions. In many ways, it is like the heart. In fact, the Old Testament scriptures often speaks of the heart and soul as if they are interchangeable. But the key distinction that makes the soul truly important and different is the component of human will—our volition and choice. The part of a son that chooses, decides his own way, can be wounded and warped. Abuse that penetrates the soul can bend it toward the will of another and a loss of freedom results. A son whose soul is wounded and overpowered will actually choose to continue in troubled and toxic relationships—not because he wants to, but because the part of him that chooses freely (his soul) has been bent and broken. It is bondage and imprisonment of the heart. The Apostle Paul said it this way: *"For I have the desire to do what is good, but I cannot carry it out. For what I do is not the good I want to do; no, the evil I do not want to do—this I keep on doing"* (Romans 7:18-19).

Personal Reflection

1. When have you felt the deepest need for a father?

2. How have you met the needs or filled the emptiness that exists because of your poor or broken relationship with your father?

3. What male relationships did you seek out in the absence of a connection with your father?

4. What is your greatest disappointment in your relationship with your father?

5. Take a few moments to honestly evaluate your relationship with your father. What comes to mind? Thank God for the times your father has been a gift to you. If you have never known your father, thank God—your heavenly Father—that he is the perfect parent.

NOTES:

CHAPTER 2

Understanding the Father-Son Wound

No one can touch a son's soul the way his father can. No one else can touch a son's feelings, shape his self-image, or move his spirit as his father can. Despite this inherent intimacy, the emotional connection between father and son is not automatic. The father has to make it happen.

Fathers have a God-given responsibility to build an emotional and spiritual bridge to their sons. Most fathers are unaware of this responsibility. And they know little about how to build such a connection.

God uses fathers to teach sons about feelings and emotions. Fathers help sons discover their feelings. Fathers model the management of those feelings through their example. Fathers enable sons to develop healthy attitudes toward women. Sons learn to respect and value the opposite sex through their fathers' influence. Fathers teach sons to care for themselves and others. Sons form values and develop principles for living by observation of their God-given example of their fathers.

Most fathers are unaware of the importance of their role. They are, therefore, unable to make a conscious effort to fulfill it. This lack of understanding and effort deepens their sons' wounds. The damage occurs not because fathers want to harm their sons. Fathers have just been unaware of their impact on their sons' lives.

When Father Doesn't Respond to His Son's Emotions

God created men with the ability to experience a full spectrum of feelings. But most men learn to deny their emotions. Young boys who haven't learned to deny their feelings express them freely. These boys hunger for their fathers to respond to the emotions they express. But instead of a heartfelt, supportive response, most boys receive rejection, cold indifference, or a harsh reaction. Imagine how this affects a boy.

To illustrate, suppose a little boy falls down, hurts himself, and begins to cry. A father's emotional response should be to embrace the boy, offer safety, and provide comfort. Such assurance tells the boy that the hurt is real and the father understands his pain. A common reaction from fathers is to scold, shame, or belittle. They might say, "What are you whimpering about? That's only a scratch!" This kind of a reaction causes fear in the boy. His body tenses, he feels shame, and he begins to program himself to ignore pain. And, most importantly, he decides never to express his pain again. The boy begins to believe that his father has no pain. He believes that he should feel no pain either.

The little boy may grow up to be a man who ignores his pain. His pain is denied until it becomes too severe for him to function. He may deny the pain until it threatens his life. Then he may require radical spiritual, medical, and psychological intervention to reverse the damage.

Or the little boy may discover that eating numbs his emotional pain. He may learn that a dozen cookies, a half-gallon of ice cream, or a bag of chips soothes his misery. As he grows, this may lead to compulsive eating. He may seek food rather than God or the support of other men. He may go through life weighing twenty, fifty, or even a hundred pounds more than he should. His overweight condition will lead to serious health problems.

An older boy may discover that alcohol numbs his inner pain. It may seem to deaden his heartache and help him function in life. Or the adolescent boy may discover that masturbation or pornography enables him to feel better for a time. All of these efforts to deaden and deny inner pain can lead a young man into compulsive, uncontrollable activities that will destroy his life.

A little boy who gets his father's emotional reaction rather than an empathetic response to his needs, may suffer for a lifetime. Other men such as uncles, grandfathers, coaches, pastors, and teachers may reinforce the father's message of emotional disapproval and rejection. Too often, older men give boys the same message: *Big boys don't cry! What happens to you really doesn't hurt!*

Of course there is a time and place to deny pain. Sometimes we must sacrifice for a larger goal. As boys become men, they need to learn when this is appropriate. For example, the pain a man endures in boot camp is a necessary part of training. Combat conditions require mental alertness and physical ability regardless of personal needs or discomfort. To respond otherwise could result in death for the man and others who depend on him.

But it is wrong for a growing boy to deny pain. It can become a way of life that devastates and destroys his health and happiness. A boy who learns to handle his pain by pushing through it may seem courageous and noble. But it renders him unable to discern his inner feelings or to respond to the feelings of others. Even the feelings of loved ones will be out of his reach.

Don, a friend of mine, was such a man. He grew up with an emotionally reactive father. Life was not easy on their small Midwestern farm. Side by side, father and son put in 12 to 14 hour days. His father gave in to physical exhaustion only on Sundays for the customary afternoon nap. But he was hard at it again on Monday—all day long. Whatever task Don was assigned, he had to complete it perfectly. No excuses.

For Don, it was a relief to enter the military after high school. Basic training was like part-time work compared to life on the farm. His training at home prepared him for the emotional rigors of military life. As a little boy, he learned to survive by extreme emotional denial. As an adult, he was emotionally detached and rarely felt the hurt that lingered deep inside.

In the service, Don discovered a source of comfort: alcohol. It made him feel better, and it gave him a feeling of camaraderie. With alcohol, he could feel a sense of belonging with the other men in his unit. He found solace and relief when he went out on liberty to drink and laugh with other men. Later in civilian life, Don found that camaraderie with his friends during the after-work happy hour. But Don's wife objected to his after-work drinking. When he was promoted to management, his former buddies no longer invited him to drink.

At this point, liquor became Don's best friend, his faithful companion. He grew closer to alcohol and more distant from his wife. Don and his wife did not communicate. They argued. He was proud of his sons, but he did not know how to have fun with them or be close to them. Don's life was limited to long hours of work, brief conversations with his neighbor, and drinking. He drank in the evenings and on the weekends. He drank while alone at home or while puttering around the garage or yard.

Don was a good man. He provided well for his wife and children. But by his early 50s, his body was worn out. He suffered a heart attack. His arteries could only carry about 20 to 25 percent of the blood his body needed. Too much food, work, and alcohol, too little exercise, too few close relationships with family and friends, and too distant a relationship with God, all took its toll on Don. An emergency triple bypass and help for his alcoholism gave him a second chance to face the emptiness he felt inside. It took life-threatening circumstances to open Don's eyes. He had become just like his father—unable to understand and respond to his feelings. His father had set the example. He knew how to work and drink, but had no idea how to be a responsive, loving friend, husband, and father.

When Father Is Absent

Every boy needs his father's active involvement in his life. Yet many sons suffer abandonment in their relationship with their fathers. Some fathers intentionally abandon their families. This is a tremendous hurt for a boy to bear. Other fathers may not abandon their families, but they are often gone from home. Still others are physically present but emotionally absent. The sons of these fathers feel abandonment in the father-son relationship.

The son, whose father completely abandons the family, suffers the deepest wound. A son may have no memory of his father. He was too young when his father left. A son may not even know his father's name. He may not have a clue about his father's identity. He would not know him if they met face to face.

These sons have a huge void—an empty hole inside. They were never able to observe their fathers. They didn't see what it meant to be a man, a husband, or a father. Often these sons have an extended family that is fragmented. Many have never seen these roles modeled by a responsible man. Learning about life comes through peers rather than through relationships with fathers, uncles, or grandfathers.

These sons also feel great shame. They wonder, *What's wrong with me? Why didn't dad want to stick around? Why doesn't he care about me? What did I do to make him go away? Why doesn't he want to know who I am?* Some of these boys may never have a meaningful relationship with any man. The father-son wound can be that deep and damaging.

Intentional permanent abandonment is a tragedy of incredible magnitude. But lesser degrees of abandonment also leave great wounds. Many fathers work 10 to 15 hours a day to build their businesses or climb the corporate ladder. A father who does this is absent during most of his son's waking hours. And the younger the son, the fewer the waking hours. Even when the father is home, he may be too tired or emotionally drained to build an emotional bridge to his son. There is no time to play, no sensitivity to listen, no energy to share himself. The son receives none of his father's strength, convictions, or values.

To the son, physical and emotional absence feels like abandonment. The son may seek out other sources—television, a favorite coach, or a gang—to find what is missing in his relationship with his father. The son also feels a certain amount of shame. He interprets his father's absence to be the result of his inadequacy or his failure to please him. These feelings may also result when a father is emotionally absent due to alcoholism, drug use, or other addictions.

An extramarital affair by a father causes another type of abandonment. When a man has an affair, he makes a clear emotional statement. His actions declare that another relationship is more important than his relationship with his family—more important than his relationship with his son. A son is devastated and often outraged. Wounded and shamed, the son usually concludes, *I don't mean anything to you!*

The father-son wound deepens if the father divorces and remarries. It is especially painful if his new wife has children who live with them. The son sees that his father cares about children who are not even his. The son only spends time with his father on weekends or during school vacations. This wound leads to jealousy and rivalry between stepchildren, and deeper distrust and feelings of shame between father and son.

When His Father Is Physically Abusive

Physical abuse by a father causes serious damage to a son. The wave of physical abuse in our society is so great that there is a movement to eliminate all corporal punishment. Physical abuse often occurs while parents discipline their children. A father may lose control and become abusive when he punishes his son. He may use physical punishment that is too harsh or severe. Some Christian fathers who are physically abusive believe they are following a biblical model of punishment. That is unfortunate and sad.

I do not recommend liberal or permissive parenting. I am all for parents who set strong limits and boundaries for their children. I support confrontation of sinful behavior. However, too many children suffer physical abuse in the name of biblical discipline. I know this is true. I have counseled with many Christian adults who endured this abuse as children. I have counseled young men who struggle with rage, depression, and various addictions—all to silence the pain of the abuse carried deep inside. I have seen adult men cry when they remember their father's "discipline." Feelings of shame and woundedness resurface. True biblical discipline does not leave abusive wounds in its wake.

Abuse by Christian fathers leaves behind more than bruises and shame. A boy may learn to avoid a particular behavior for which he is punished. He may also be confused about his relationship with his parents and with God. A boy who has been physically abused by his father also may view God as abusive. He may fear that God will become violently angry with him. He may fear that God is waiting for an excuse to pour his wrath and judgment down upon him.

When His Father Reacts with Rage or Shame

Rage is a type of emotional abuse. The damage suffered through a father's emotional abuse is similar to the results from his physical abuse. In both emotional and physical abuse, a boy feels shame. He emotionally distances himself from his father. A boy also learns to deny his feelings. He may engage in behaviors that insulate him from his emotional pain.

Some fathers emotionally abuse their sons by reacting with rage to their son's mistakes. For instance, a boy may accidently break a window while playing ball. A father wounds his son when he responds with rage and yells at him in front of his friends. The boy may channel the pain of his father's rage into effort to become a great baseball player. Or he may be afraid to risk anything. The boy may live in fear that something bad will happen to him if he makes a mistake or neglects to do thing just right.

In scripture, King Saul raged at his son, Jonathan, when Jonathan foiled Saul's plan to murder David. Notice the rage and shame in the interaction between father and son:

> Then Saul said to his son Jonathan, "Why hasn't the son of Jesse come to the meal, either yesterday or today?"
>
> Jonathan answered, "David earnestly asked me for permission to go to Bethlehem. He said, 'Let me go, because our family is observing a sacrifice in the town and my brother has ordered me to be there. If I have found favor in your eyes, let me get away to see my brothers.' That is why he has not come to the king's table."
>
> Saul's anger flared up at Jonathan and he said to him, "You son of a perverse and rebellious woman! Don't I know that you have sided with the son of Jesse to your own shame and to the shame of the mother who bore you? As long as the son of Jesse lives on this earth, neither you nor your kingdom will be established. Now send and bring him to me, for he must die!"
>
> "Why should he be put to death? What has he done?" Jonathan asked his father. But Saul hurled his spear at him to kill him. Then Jonathan knew that his father intended to kill David. Jonathan got up from the table in fierce anger... (1 Samuel 20:27-34).

This is not normal dinnertime conversation. Saul rages at Jonathan, humiliates him, insults him, taunts him, and even tries to kill him. Scripture doesn't tell us how this interaction affected Jonathan's heart, but we can be sure it made a deep impact. Rage always shames a son, and shame is a deep wound.

An old Jewish proverb says to shame a man publically is like shedding his blood. Shame is one of the deep wounds men receive from their fathers, from society, and from the Christian community. Many men have deep layers of shame that insulate them from their feelings.

Shame occurs when a father rages at his son. It also occurs during the daily interaction between father and son. A son is shamed when his father says, "Oh, grow up! Big boys don't cry. That's nothing to cry about!" A son also is humiliated by his father's drunkenness. If a father is drunk in front of a boy's friends or in public, the son is humiliated. A son's shame grows deeper with every broken promise. When a father fails to attend a promised ball game, shame grows. A son is shamed when his father notices his imperfections or failures more than his accomplishments. A son is shamed when his father expects him to accomplish tasks for which he has had no instruction. And a son is shamed by the physical or sexual abuse of his father.

When a son is blasted with his father's rage or shame, his only option is to do what Jonathan did—leave. Any emotional bridge that exists between father and son is destroyed by abuse and shame. The son cannot talk reasonably with his father. If he cannot physically leave his father, as Jonathan did, he will emotionally disconnect with him.

When His Father Is Sexually Abusive

Sexual abuse is one of the deepest wounds a boy can suffer. Estimates indicate that one out of every six men has been sexually abused. I believe those figures are low because sexual abuse is difficult for men to talk about. All sexual abuse is damaging. But it is most damaging when a boy's father has been the abuser.

Sexual abuse by the father fragments a boy. It is a violation of a boy's whole being. He is torn apart emotionally, spiritually, and physically. He is left with a lifelong sense of shame. He believes that he is a bad person. Often, an abusive father tells a boy that the sexual abuse is punishment. Many times, the abuse is so traumatic that a boy blocks its from his memory.

Sexual abuse by the father has a lifelong impact on a boy. The father plays the major role in shaping his son's view of sexuality. Sexual abuse from the father creates confusion in the boy's sexual orientation. The father's abuse makes all men appear to be dangerous. But it also creates a deep attraction for close relationships with other men as a result of the boy's hunger for his father's true affection.

It is not uncommon for a boy who has been sexually abused by his father to become a homosexual. Other men who have been sexually abused may turn toward pornography, and other forms of sexual addiction. Even if he pursues heterosexual relationships, he often feels physically inadequate. And he has difficulty communicating within those relationships.

A father's covert forms of sexual abuse leave deep wounds, too. A father's pornographic material exposes a son to a distorted view of sexuality and women. A father's disrespectful sexual comments about women communicate a distorted view of masculine sexuality. A father's comments about a woman's breast size misplaces a woman's value. A father's references to a woman as a whore or slut conveys disrespect. A father who looks at all women in a sexual way distorts his son's view of masculinity and femininity.

A father who is passive or silent about sexuality also wounds his son. A father has a responsibility to nurture his son's developing sexuality. Without a father's instruction, a son learns about sexuality from friends, television, movies, books, magazines, and the Internet. This is not the way God intended a young man to develop his sexual identity.

Covert or Emotional Incest in the Home

The primary relationship in the family exists between the husband and wife. God designed the family to operate that way. But troubled marriages lack the needed spiritual and emotional bond. In this case, the primary relationship often exists between children and parents. When this kind of relationship exists between child and parent rather than husband and wife, we call it covert or emotional incest. Covert incest devastates the father-son relationship. It is one of the most common forms of emotional and sexual abuse today.

Kenneth Adams aptly describes the devastating impact of covert incest:

> Covert incest occurs when a child becomes the object of a parent's affection, love, passion and preoccupation. The parent, motivated by the loneliness and emptiness created by a chronically troubled marriage or relationship, makes the child a surrogate partner. The boundary between caring and incestuous love is crossed when the relationship with the child exists to meet the needs of the parent rather than those of the child. As the deterioration in the marriage progresses, the dependency on the child grows and the opposite-sex parent's response to the child becomes increasingly characterized by desperation, jealousy, and a disregard for personal boundaries. The child becomes an object to be manipulated and used so the parent can avoid the pain and reality of a troubled marriage.
>
> The child feels used and trapped, the same feelings overt incest victims experience. Attempts at play, autonomy and friendship render the child guilt-ridden and lonely, never able to feel okay about his or her needs. Over time, the child becomes preoccupied with the parent's needs and feels protective and concerned. A psychological marriage between parent and child results. The child becomes the parent's surrogate spouse.
>
> ...An important difference between overt and covert incest is that, while the overt victim feels abused, the covert victim feels idealized and privileged. Yet underneath the thin mask of feeling special and privileged rests the same trauma of the overt victim: rage, anger, shame and guilt.... The adult covert incest victim remains stuck in a pattern of living aimed at keeping the special relationships going with the opposite-sex parent. It is a pattern of always trying to please Mommy or Daddy.[1]

The symptoms of covert incest are not difficult to recognize. Most of them apply to adult children as well as younger children:

❑ The parent looks toward the child for emotional support that is not provided by the spouse.

❑ The child is the primary source of the parent's emotional support.

❑ The parent would rather spend time with the child than with the spouse.

❑ The parent shares angry, critical feelings with the child concerning the spouse.

❑ The parent's happiness rises and falls with the child's accomplishments.

❑ The parent becomes resentful or jealous of the child's happiness or accomplishments.

❑ The child is afraid or worried that the parent's marriage will fail unless he or she supports the parents.

❑ The child worries about what might happen if he or she is not available to meet the parent's needs.

❑ The married child is closer and more emotionally supportive of his or her parent than his or her spouse.

❑ The child feels that he or she exists for the parent's needs. When the parent does not reciprocate, the child feels used or manipulated.

❑ The parent provides emotional support and encouragement for the child, but does not provide such support for the spouse.

The Bible provides a remarkable example of the impact covert incest can have on a family, particularly its impact on the father-son relationship. The story begins in Genesis 25, and concerns the relationship of Isaac and Rebekah and their twin sons, Jacob and Esau.

We see conflict in this family from its beginning. Even before birth, the twins struggled against each other (Genesis 25:22-25). As the boys matured, each parent chose a favorite. The Bible says, "Esau became a skillful hunter, a man of the open country, while Jacob was a quiet man, staying among the tents. Isaac, who had a taste for wild game, loved Esau, but Rebekah loved Jacob" (Genesis 25:27-28). As the firstborn, Esau had the right to receive the primary blessing from this father. But Scripture says Esau "despised his birthright" (Genesis 25:34). He returned home hungry from a futile hunting trip and sold his birthright to his younger brother in exchange for stew (Genesis 25:29-34). Notice that Jacob did not just take Esau's word for the exchange: "But Jacob said, 'Swear to me first.' So he swore an oath to him, selling his birthright to Jacob" (Genesis 25:33).

Betrayal and a lack of trust was also evident in the relationship between the parents. In Genesis 26:1-10, we learn that Isaac put Rebekah at great personal risk to save his own neck. During a time of famine, God had promised to protect and bless Isaac and his descendants. God told him exactly where to live (vs. 2-6). However, "When the men of that place asked him about his wife, he said, 'She is my sister,' because he was afraid to say, 'She is my wife.' He thought, 'The men of this place might kill me on account of Rebekah, because she is beautiful'" (v.7). Later, the king was horrified to learn what Isaac had done. He said, "What is this you have done to us? One of the men might well have slept with your wife, and you would have brought guilt upon us" (v.10).

Isaac's self-protective lie put Rebekah at great physical, emotional, and spiritual risk. Even though he had a promise of safety from God, he rejected the opportunity to live by faith. Instead, he responded in fear and betrayed his wife. It's interesting that Isaac's father, Abraham, did the same thing on two different occasions. When faced with similar circumstances, Abraham also claimed that his wife was his sister (see Genesis 12:10-20; 20:1-16). The histories of many families reveal a repetition of the same problems generation after generation. It takes courage to change and to do what no man in your family has done. Isaac was unable to take that courageous step of faith. Like his father, he chose to put his wife at great personal risk.

It is my opinion that Isaac's actions created a wound in his relationship with Rebekah. That wound never healed. I believe it contributed to the covert incest that shattered the family and led to brokenness in the father-son relationships. The wound Rebekah felt in her marital relationship was played out through her children many years later:

> When Isaac was old and his eyes weak, he called for Esau his older son and said to him, "My son."
> "Here I am," he answered.
> Isaac said, "I am now an old man and don't know the day of

my death. Now then, get your weapon — your quiver and bow —
and go out to the open country to hunt some wild game for me.
Prepare me the kind of tasty food I like and bring it to me to eat,
so that I may give you my blessing before I die" (Genesis 27:1-4).

Now Rebekah listened as Isaac spoke to his son Esau. When
Esau left for the open country to hunt game and bring it back,
Rebekah said to her son Jacob:

> Look, I overheard your father say to your brother Esau,
> "Bring me some game and prepare me some tasty food to eat, so
> that I may give you my blessing in the presence of the Lord be-
> fore I die." Now, my son, listen carefully and do what I tell you:
> Go out to the flock and bring me two choice young goats, so I
> can prepare some tasty food for your father, just the way he likes
> it. Then take it to your father to eat, so that he may give you his
> blessing before he dies (Genesis 27:6-10).

Jacob expressed concern about being caught in such deception. But his mother assured him she would prepare the food and
disguise him. Isaac would never know he was blessing Jacob rather
than Esau. When Isaac questioned whether or not the son before
him truly was Esau, Jacob lied and said he was. Together, Jacob
and Rebekah succeeded in deceiving Isaac (see Genesis 27:11-29).

The fact that Rebekah would even think of such deception indicates that the spiritual and emotional bond between husband and
wife had been broken. That Jacob would even consider her plot
indicates a strong emotional bond between mother and son. Jacob
had begun to view his father through his mother's eyes. The
father-son relationship was clearly damaged. The fact that Jacob
could openly lie to his father indicates his lack of respect for him.
But there's more:

> After Isaac finished blessing him and Jacob had scarcely
> left his father's presence, his brother Esau came in from hunting.
> He too prepared some tasty food and brought it to his father.
> Then he said to him, "My father, sit up and eat some of my game,
> so that you may give me your blessing."
> His father Isaac asked him, "Who are you?"

"I am your son," he answered, "your firstborn, Esau."

Isaac trembled violently and said, "Who was it, then, that hunted game and brought it to me? I ate it just before you came and I blessed him—and indeed he will be blessed!"

When Esau heard his father's words, he burst out with a loud and bitter cry and said to his father, "Bless me—me too, my father!"

But he said, "Your brother came deceitfully and took your blessing."

Esau said, "Isn't he rightly named Jacob? He has deceived me these two times: He took my birthright, and now he's taken my blessing!" Then he asked, "Haven't you reserved any blessing for me?"

Isaac answered Esau, "I have made him lord over you and have made all his relatives his servants, and I have sustained him with grain and new wine. So what can I possibly do for you, my son?"

Esau said to his father, "Do you have only one blessing, my father? Bless me too, my father!" Then Esau wept aloud (Genesis 27:30-38).

It is easy to feel the deep pain both Isaac and Esau are suffering. Together they realize what Rebekah and her accomplice Jacob have taken from them.

Isaac realizes that he has been betrayed. His own son has lied to him. He is so enraged that he is trembling. Perhaps he suspects that Rebekah had something to do with these events. She finally got back at him for her deep-seated anger about what he had done to her years earlier.

Esau is devastated. He had waited his whole life for the day of his father's blessing. To be blessed by his father is a very special moment in a man's life. The father's blessing conveys his unchangeable approval and acceptance of his son as a man. Yet Esau had been robbed of the most meaningful event in his life. Feeling the loss, he repeatedly asked his father for a blessing—any blessing. His anguished cry of deep sadness and loss is undeniable.

Jacob, on the other hand, accomplished his mother's wishes. He received the blessing he wanted, but he paid a tremendous price. He shattered whatever relationship he had with his brother. Their relationship would remain that way for much of his life. But more importantly, by deceiving his father, Jacob loses the benefit of a relationship with him. By stealing his father's blessing for Esau, Jacob misses out on whatever experiences or blessing his father would have shared with him. Jacob does not cry about his loss as Esau did, but it is nonetheless painful.

All sons need the blessing of a deep and meaningful relationship with their fathers. Grandsons of the patriarch Abraham, sons of farmers, or sons of corporate giants—all boys need to be emotionally connected with their fathers. To fully grow into manhood, all boys need the heartfelt love and intimate involvement of their fathers. Without this connection, they bear a father-son wound that affects every aspect of their lives. When enough men are wounded in this way, the whole society changes.

A Closer Look

Abuse—A simple understanding of abuse is the violation of a boundary. A controlling or manipulative parent or spouse causes abuse. Rage, volume, and physical intimidation may cause abuse. Disrespectful and demeaning language is abusive. Inappropriate touching or sexual contact with a child is abuse. Inappropriate emotional dependence upon a child is abusive. Unrealistic expectations placed upon a child can cause abuse. And of course, neglect of a child's needs is abusive.

Fear—Fear is a gift from God. Without it we would walk into traffic or place ourselves in danger. But fear often becomes our first response to anything new. We meet change with fear because we feel threatened by so many things. Fear creates a physical response that begins with the release of adrenaline and ends up with the whole body on alert. This alerted state often leads to persistent and unwanted tension and can develop into stress-related illness.

Shame—Shame is different from guilt. Guilt is a God-given response to a violation of our conscience. Guilt says that we did wrong. But shame is humiliation. It makes us feel as though *we*—not just our actions—are wrong. Shame pulls away the fig leaf and exposes our nakedness and weakness and imperfections. Shame is a cruel, emotional spotlight on the vulnerable and private parts of our lives. It is often used as an abusive tool to control and manipulate others.

Covert or Emotional Incest—This form of incest occurs when a parent turns to his or her child, rather than to the spouse, for emotional support. In this case, a child becomes the object of a parent's affection, love, passion and preoccupation. The parent, motivated by the loneliness and emptiness created by a chronically troubled marriage or relationship, makes the child a surrogate partner.

Personal Reflection

1. Which wounds in your life today have resulted from your relationship with your father?

2. If you could encourage your father to initiate an emotional connection with you, what would that connection be like?

3. How has your relationship with your father impacted your self-image?

4. What losses in your relationship with your father have been most difficult or painful for you?

5. Did either of your parents succumb to covert or emotional incest with you or a sibling? Describe the relationship.

NOTES:

CHAPTER 3

The Father-Son Wound and Society

A son gains a solid, personal foundation that will last a lifetime when a true emotional bond occurs between father and son. A son gains a sense of his personal identity from the connection with his father. He also acquires his core values. He develops solid convictions. He attains a sense of purpose. And he discovers a masculine strength that he can draw upon during difficult times.

The tragedy of our time is that most men have not had this fundamental, emotional bond with their fathers. The result is a loss of masculine intimacy. Men do not know how to connect with other men. The loss has yielded tragic results.

Today, young men in their late teens and 20s seem overwhelmed and unable to discover direction and purpose in their lives. This can be a normal developmental stage. But the young men I counsel hunger for guidance and direction from older men. Unfortunately, most of these young men lack relationships with fathers, grandfathers, uncles, or elders at church. They have no one to whom they can turn for insight and advice.

The lack of an older man's influence affects many areas of a young man's life. One major area is work and the development of a work ethic. Many young men do not understand the concept of paying one's dues in the workplace—starting at the bottom and working toward the top. They do not understand what it means to take on responsibility and carry a job through to completion. When the job gets too hard or uncomfortable, they want to bail out.

Perhaps the most devastating problem today is the lack of a

moral foundation. Without strong moral character a young man's life is built on shifting sand. Many cannot imagine waiting until marriage to have sex. The idea of a lifelong relationship with one woman is foreign. Sex has become casual. No commitment or long-term relationship necessary. Sex today is like hand holding was thirty years ago. The blame cannot fall on only the young men. The strong, moral values that our society once had have not been passed down to today's young men.

The loss of masculine intimacy also affects men in their 30s and 40s. The difficult years of mid-life cause a man to draw upon the inner resources. They hope to find an inner strength that will carry them through. But most men find nothing. They are empty deep inside. There is no inner strength upon which to draw—no unshakable values or convictions.

Many men in mid-life have no experience of masculine closeness or support. Most have no close relationships with older men to whom they can turn for wisdom. They have no older men to kindle their courage and summon their strength.

A sad symptom of the loss of masculine connection is the lack of commitment to marriage and family. Men in mid-life find it all too easy to betray their marriages and have an affair. The illusion of a more satisfying relationship causes them to abandon their marriages.

Even the older men bear the painful consequences of broken father-son relationships. They have survived many difficulties in life and endured hardships alone. The strength of a healthy bond with other men was never there. They then cannot recognize the influence, power, and responsibility they could offer younger men. They cannot understand the need to affirm and support them. They do not take seriously their leadership role in the church and community. Many older men are content to golf, fish, and bowl. They cannot see the value they could contribute to society.

The State of Men Today

The loss of masculine intimacy is tragic for individual men and society at large. Examples of the breakdown of basic values in our society are everywhere. The wound in father-son relationships has added to the failure of the family. It has contributed to the loss of Christian influence in our culture. It has corroded confidence in our leaders at all levels of society. It has deepened the moral vacuum in our cities. We see riots in the streets and disrespect for authority. We hear of scandals in our financial institutions and a lack of integrity among our elected officials. And beyond our view there is an ever-increasing number of abortions.

The changes that have taken place in society are dramatic. James Patterson and Peter Kim, authors of *The Day America Told the Truth: What People Really Believe About Everything That Really Matters*[1], compiled a new set of "commandments." They say that these are now the rules by which American society now lives. They have concluded that no moral consensus exists in America today. Instead, individuals make up their own moral code. Patterson and Kim base the commandments they have compiled on numerous surveys they have conducted among men and women of all ages.

Today's Ten Commandments

1. I don't see the point of observing the Sabbath (77 percent).
2. I will steal from those who won't really miss it (74 percent).
3. I will lie when it suits me, so long as it does not cause any real damage (64 percent).
4. I will drink and drive if I feel that I can handle it. I know my limit (56 percent).
5. I will cheat on my spouse—after all, given the chance, he or she will do the same (53 percent).
6. I will procrastinate at work and do absolutely nothing about one full day in every five. It is standard operating procedure (50 percent).
7. I will use recreational drugs (41 percent).
8. I will cheat on my taxes—to a point (30 percent).
9. I will put my lover at risk of disease. I sleep around a bit, but who doesn't (31 percent).
10. Technically, I may have committed date rape, but I know that she wanted it (20 percent have been date raped).[2]

What a difference between these commandments and the ones God gave to Moses on Mt. Sinai! Notice the contrasts:

And God spoke all these words:

"I am the LORD your God, who brought you out of Egypt, out of the land of slavery.

"You shall have no other gods before me.

"You shall not make for yourself an idol in the form of anything in heaven above or on the earth beneath or in the waters below.

You shall not bow down to them or worship them; for I, the LORD your God, am a jealous God, punishing the children for the sin of the fathers to the third and fourth generation of those who hate me, but showing love to a thousand generations of those who love me and keep my commandments.

"You shall not misuse the name of the LORD your God, for the LORD will not hold anyone guiltless who misuses his name.

"Remember the Sabbath day by keeping it holy.

Six days you shall labor and do all your work, but the seventh day is a Sabbath to the LORD your God. On it you shall not do any work, neither you, nor your son or daughter, nor your manservant or maidservant, nor your animals, nor the alien within your gates.

For in six days the LORD made the heavens and the earth, the sea, and all that is in them, but he rested on the seventh day. Therefore the LORD blessed the Sabbath day and made it holy.

"Honor your father and your mother, so that you may live long in the land the LORD your God is giving you.

"You shall not murder.

"You shall not commit adultery.

"You shall not steal.

"You shall not give false testimony against your neighbor.

"You shall not covet your neighbor's house. You shall not covet your neighbor's wife, or his manservant or maidservant, his ox or donkey, or anything that belongs to your neighbor" (Exodus 20:1-17).

The contrast between the Ten Commandments and the new commandments summarized by Patterson and Kim are alarming. Scripture makes clear statements about right and wrong. But there is no clear definition of right and wrong in our culture today. Scripture declares that there is only one God. It also states that God's day is holy. Our culture asserts that God does not matter. Every day is our own to use as we choose. The "shall nots" of Scripture have become the "I won't unless I want to's" of society. The vacuum of moral belief is obvious.

The Ten Commandments listed in Exodus are the foundational rules on which our society was built. Our religious beliefs—or lack of beliefs—do not add to or detract from the truth of the Commandments. These commandments are a true standard of conduct for society. They teach the difference between right and wrong. By them, we know that it is wrong to steal, to lie, to murder, to commit adultery, and to want whatever belongs to our neighbor.

A generation or two ago, the Ten Commandments were still the fundamental guidelines by which American men lived. But those guidelines have not been passed down to young men today. Our society has lost the strong foundation of biblical values that is necessary for our survival. We have discarded our only rock-solid foundation—God's word. Society has chosen the shaky and sinking sand of today's shifting morality. These are frightening times. Our culture, our families, and our government are at risk.

The new commandments summarized by Patterson and Kim expose the breakdown of community and family relationships. They reveal the inner struggles of adults from dysfunctional families. They also reveal the great wound that has been created in the souls of children. It is the spiritual, emotional, and at times physical absence of fathers in their lives. The new commandments uncover the many substitutes that are used to fill the void in the father-son relationship. They reveal the frantic, unchecked pursuit of something—anything—to fill the vacuum of the lost connection with father. This loss—this deep need—has changed the moral code of our society.

Patterson and Kim have more research that reveals even greater disintegration of fundamental values:

▶93 percent said that they, and no one, else determine what is and what is not moral.

▶84 percent confessed that they would violate the established rules of their religion.

▶When asked what beliefs they would die for, 48 percent said, "none."

▶Nearly half the population honestly feel that nobody knows them.

▶30 percent believe their mothers know them and 19 percent believe their fathers know them.

▶50 percent of 18 to 24 year-olds honestly feel they received a good moral foundation from their parents.

▶Lying has become a cultural trait in America, 91 percent of us lie regularly.

▶Only 29 percent of Americans are virgins when they marry.

▶92 percent of sexually active people report having had 10 or more lovers.

▶Almost one-third of all married Americans (31 percent) have had or are having an affair.

▶62 percent of those having affairs believe there is nothing morally wrong with what they are doing.

▶Among 18 to 24 year olds, 61 percent revealed that they had lost their virginity by age sixteen; one in five kids report doing so by age 13.

▶One in six adults across America were physically abused during childhood; one in seven adults were sexually abused (remember, most do not tell).

▶One in four women will be sexually assaulted.

▶As many as one in 20 Americans have participated in some ritual of Satanism or witchcraft.

▶There is practically no sense of community anywhere in America today.

▶25 percent of Americans believe they will be divorced within the next five years.[3]

Fundamental changes have occurred in the ethical and moral beliefs of people today. The changes are frightening because they are subtle. Most of us are unaware of them until they have produced tragic circumstances. Then we are struck by the blow. In disbelief we watch young people massacre their fellow students. We see children afraid to go to school because of the violence.

The breakup of the family has contributed to the demise of traditional, fundamentally biblical values in American society. Nearly two out of three children no longer grow up in the same family in which they were born. Children are terribly confused. Families break up and form new families. Children have to deal with the dysfunction of four (or more) families of origin rather than just two. No wonder children have trouble bonding with their parents and accepting their values.

The church is no longer the center of community and social life. This adds to loss of biblical values in society. Today people no longer depend on the church for their social activities. So many other options exist. The church no longer leads the community in charity and help for the needy. Today people rely on government to meet their needs. To many people, the church appears irrelevant in our society.

The tragic state of society today is, in part, a result of the lack of spiritual and emotional intimacy between fathers and their children—particularly their sons. This lack of emotional connection between father and son has a devastating impact on men in every stage of life, and on every level of society. How is it possible for one relationship to have such a powerful impact? The father-son relationship is the most formative relationship in a man's life. The father-son relationship directs the development of the son's masculine identity. It is the main avenue to convey the guiding principles and values of life. It is how they are passed from one generation to the next. When the father is not emotionally connected to his son, his son lacks trust in his father and his father's values judgment, emotions, and spirituality.

I am not alone in my assessment. Storyteller and poet Robert Bly, researcher and motivational business speaker Stephen R. Covey, and pastor Gordon Dalbey have all written about the father-son wound and its impact on masculine identity and behavior. Their findings and insights provide a helpful perspective on the societal impact of the father-son wound.

A Loss of Intimacy and Emotional Bonding

Robert Bly understands the issues men face today. He believes that the industrial revolution brought about a fundamental change in father-son relationships. And the change was not good. Much was lost. Prior to the industrial revolution, most fathers and sons worked side by side in the fields. In the cities, sons learned a trade or a skill from their fathers. Fathers and sons had consistent contact. They worked together for the family's survival.

Something special happens when a son works side by side with his father. An emotional connection takes place that's beyond description. The time that a father and son spend time together deepens the bond between them. That connection provides a foundation for the boy's developing personality. Of course, the boy is wounded if the father is shaming or abusive. But the boy is nurtured if the father is able to express his feelings and respond to his son's feelings. Healthy side-by-side contact between father and son feeds the boy at a deep emotional level.

The industrial revolution brought automation and great factories. Men moved from fields to assembly lines and offices. Sons no longer worked with their fathers. In fact, most sons no longer saw their fathers at work and rarely saw their workplace. Families no longer worked together in unity to survive. Men spent less time at home with their children. Mothers became the emotional center of the family. Fathers grew more distant from the family.

A business man develops skills and methods of dealing with people and their problems. These tactics can make a man successful in his profession. Yet theses techniques for business rarely work in the home. Consider the following examples:

An engineer thinks in ways that are objective, factual, and concrete. Facts, figures, charts, and graphs are his life. His mind-set and skills make him an excellent financial planner. He will provide well for his family's future needs. But it can be difficult for an engineer to respond to the feelings of his family members. At work he wrestles with reasons and facts. At home he faces a family with emotional needs.

An attorney is trained to argue his case. He is a master of debate and tactical strategies. He uses words to gain advantage over an adversary. He poses key questions to establish his argument. But the cunning litigator is not needed at home. Family relationships require sensitivity and tenderness. At home, emotions can run high and feelings get hurt. A lawyer's wife and children do not need a rigid, calculating competitor. They need a caring husband and father.

A machinist works with the same machines all day long. He deals with precise tolerances to the hundredths or thousandths of inches. That standard of perfection is not necessary at home. No one in his family can be, or cares to be, that precise. Yet he may have no tolerance for any deviation to his prescribed expectations. He may have no ability to deal with the fuzzy nature of feelings. Emotions are not easy to control.

A pastor's duties range from spiritual leadership to administration, pastoral counseling, and fund-raising. People expect him to offer spiritual advice for a host of problems. But the need at home is for his personal and emotional response. Pastoral duties may leave him burned out and overwhelmed. All day long he deals with the demands of parishioners and people in need. He may come home with no energy left for his family. They need his emotion involvement and his positive feelings. But he may have given his best all day long. So his family gets the leftovers: his anger, frustration, and fatigue.

It takes wisdom and flexibility for a father to transition from work to home. At home he must lay down the weapons of the workplace. He must engage and follow his heart for his family's sake. His workplace skills help him accomplish his goals and achieve success in the world. But his ability to emotionally connect will gain him intimacy in his family relationships. At home he must learn to understand and communicate through the language of the heart.

There is no substitute for an intimate, emotional connection between father and son. This connection cannot be made by a father who is physically or emotionally absent. It cannot be made by a father who functions the same way at home as he does in the workplace. It takes time and emotional involvement for a father to establish intimacy with his son.

A New Ethic

The new commandments summarized earlier in this chapter illustrate how society's values have changed during the past few generations. The research of Stephen R. Covey helps us understand how and why this change has taken place.

Covey studied what people had written about success in the past 200 years. He discovered an ethical change in society over the last 50 years of the 20th Century. Prior to World War II, a person's character was of utmost importance in achieving success. Since that time, however, a person's personality has become the key to success.

Success literature written 50 to 200 years ago emphasized a person's character. The important qualities that Covey describes are "integrity, humility, fidelity, temperance, courage, justice, patience, industry, simplicity, modesty, and the Golden Rule."[4] Since then, however, writing about success focuses on "social image consciousness, techniques and quick fixes — with social band-aids and aspirin that addressed acute problems and sometimes even appeared to solve them temporarily but left the underlying chronic problems untouched to fester and resurface time and again."[5]

In the new ethic, personality has become more important than character. Success comes to the person with the right public image, behaviors, skills, and techniques. Appearances and impressions outweigh virtue and integrity. The man on the outside supercedes the person on the inside.

This fundamental change has had a tremendous impact on both the family and father-son relationships. The personality ethic enables people to be "successful" without any real substance on the inside. A person can appear successful, yet be a total failure in every significant relationship in life. A man can seem to do the impossible on the job, but be unresponsive to the emotional pain of his son. A man may have a high-profile position at work, but have no depth of core values to live by or to pass on to his children.

Those who live by a personality ethic experience the common struggles of relationships and families. But they seek the easy solutions over the right solutions. For example, if sexual needs are not met in the marriage, it is easier to have an affair. It's too difficult to search out and deal with the source of the problem. It is much easier to abandon a relationship than to resolve recurring difficulties. The values of fidelity or lifelong commitment in marriage are outdated. The character traits our society once valued are now passe´.

The new personality ethic yields tragic results in father-son relationships. Strong character values that were passed down from father to son are lost. A son may notice that his father does whatever is necessary to be successful in business. He may see that his father is unconcerned that his actions are unethical. Expediency is what matters. He may see that his father has the right haircut, the right suits, and the right car. And he may also notice that his father has little initiative or interest for his son's world. A son may hear his father talk about a commitment to God, but see that his father is a little too friendly with the neighbor's wife. He may hear his father talk about how he cheats on his taxes. A father who lives by the personality ethic has little strength of character to pass on to his son.

The lack of commitment fostered by the personality ethic also contributes to the breakup and abandonment of families by fathers. Sons get even less time with their fathers. Today, 50 percent of all fathering is done on an every-other-weekend basis. Growing children can no longer count on both parents being a part of their lives. I have no desire to single out or shame fathers in this situation. I want to create an awareness of the impact of broken father-son relationships. Fathers can take steps to curb this destructive trend. And they must do whatever is necessary to build emotionally intimate relationships with their sons.

The Television Image of Tough Masculinity

Changes in society have diminished the emotional bridge between the grandfather, father, and son. For the first time, a generation of people have a moral code primarily developed by television. Heroes from television, video games, movies, and sports fill the void that God intended a father to fill in a boy's life. These characters become his models and mentors. They shape his identity and dictate his values.

I am not exaggerating the influence that television has on a boy's development. I regularly counsel men who did not have deep and meaningful relationships with their fathers. In the absence of a father-son relationship, they adopted the masculine values and images that they saw on television. One young sex addict in his early 30s could not imagine living faithfully with only one woman during his lifetime. His main idea of love and romance had come from the "Loveboat." It took months of therapy before he began to realize that not everyone has sex before marriage. This was a totally new concept for him to consider.

Warren Farrell, author of *The Liberated Man*, has written about the standard of masculinity in our television-oriented culture. Farrell refers to John Wayne as the "Moses of Masculinity." He portrays him with a tablet that lists the "ten commandments" of traditional maledom:

1. Thou shalt not cry or expose other feelings of emotion, fear, weakness, sympathy, empathy or involvement before thy neighbor.
2. Thou shalt not be vulnerable, but honor and respect the "logical," "practical," or "intellectual"—as thou definest them.
3. Thou shalt not listen except to find fault.
4. Thou shalt condescend to women in the smallest and biggest of ways.
5. Thou shalt control thy wife's body.
6. Thou shalt have no other egos before thee.
7. Thou shalt have no other breadwinners before thee.
8. Thou shalt not be responsible for housework—before anybody.
9. Thou shalt honor and obey the straight and narrow pathway to success: job specialization.
10. Thou shalt have an answer to all problems at all times.[6]

These commandments summarize the standards of the "tough man." He faces the most challenging issues with no hint of fear. He bears the greatest pain without flinching. Like John Wayne, the tough man only shows pain when he is shot—then he grits his teeth and defeats the bad guy anyway.

These rules exact a harsh toll upon men. They impact the quality and quantity of a man's life:

▶ Men live, on the average, almost 10 years less than women;
▶ Males commit suicide 300 percent more often;
▶ All the major diseases leading toward death show significantly higher rates for males;
▶ Men have higher murder and assault and battery rates; and
▶ Men show a significantly higher rate of drug and alcohol abuse.[7]

There can be no doubt that the masculine values and images portrayed on television are detrimental to men. There is also no doubt that young boys soak up these values. The tragedy is not that television images are of such poor quality. The tragedy is that when fathers do not bond with their sons, their sons fill that void with whatever they can find.

Boys will always find heroes. When those heroes are cartoon or movie characters, boys soak up the values, attitudes, and fantasies projected on the screen. If the boy's hero is his coach, he will soak up the "tough man" values and attitudes that the coach projects. When a father is not emotionally connected with his son, these are the models that will influence his son's sexual identity. These are the models that define his sense of right and wrong. These models form his idea of what life is about. They provide his concept of how relationships work.

The Untapped Strength of Men

Men have powerful and positive roles to play in both family and society. But most of the strength that men have to offer is untapped. I am excited about the spiritual, emotional, and relational strength that resides in the fellowship of Christian men. They can provide a significant resource in the community. But most Christian men are an underdeveloped resource. Most Christian men are unaware of their own father-son wound. So they remain its victims. That deep, unhealed hurt holds every aspect of a man's life hostage. His career, his family life, and his spiritual life are all affected.

Society, the church, and individual families need Christian men to realize their potential and fulfill their God-given responsibilities. That will begin to happen when men recognize the impact of the father-son wound and when they take steps to heal that wound.

A Closer Look

Personality Ethic — The new personality ethic reflects a change in how our society measures success. 50 to 200 hundred years ago, society emphasized a person's character. Integrity, humility, fidelity, temperance, courage, justice, patience, industry, simplicity, modesty, and the Golden Rule were the standards. Today, success is about appearance and image. People can be successful without any real substance on the inside. A person can appear successful, yet be a total failure in every significant relationship in life.

Television-Oriented Culture — Television can fill the void left by the loss of emotional bonds between the grandfather, father, and son. A generation of people have a moral code primarily developed by television. Heros from television, video games, movies, and sports fill the void that God intended a boy's father to fill. Fantastic and fictitious characters become his models and mentors. They shape his identity and dictate his values.

Personal Reflection

1. In what way has the personality ethic affected the way you conduct your life?

2. Did your father allow his business demeanor and attitude to seep into family life? In what ways? In what ways do you bring the workplace home?

3. Describe the impact of television morality upon yourself and your family.

4. Who were your heroes during childhood? In what ways did you look up to your father? Grandfather? Uncles?

5. Who are your closest friends? Do you regularly fellowship with Christian men? Who provides the most positive influence in your life? Do you know your son's friends? What influences are shaping him?

NOTES:

CHAPTER 4

The Father-Son Wound and Family Life

When a man reaches his 20s, he sets out to make his place in the world. It is an exciting time for him. Many aspects of his life begin to change. He directs his energy into building his career. And, if he is married, he puts energy into his marriage.

He soon feels the burden of his family's financial needs. He may work 50 to 70 hours a week to provide the best of everything for the family he loves. He may jump through hoop after hoop to meet his need for achievement and to gain financial security for his family.

A man who is compelled to achieve and provide has little time for friends. There is no time to maintain close, caring friendships. He has no room to develop relationships with older men. He forfeits the wisdom and support they could give a young husband and father. He foregoes the guidance and direction they could give him in his career. His energies are focused on priorities rather than relationships.

This is a dangerous time for a young man. Every man needs close relationships with other men. Trouble lies ahead for the young man who lacks these relationships. The father-wound in his heart can only be filled through relationships with other men and with God. The painful emptiness a man feels inside will seek comfort.

A man may seek to fill that masculine wound through relationships with women. But women cannot meet this deep emotional need. A man who shares his deeper feelings only with women is in emotionally dangerous waters. He is headed for stormy seas. His marriage and family will suffer.

Most men, at this period of life, have not become aware of their father-son wound. This puts them at risk. They are disconnected from their feelings. They are out of touch from the grief, emptiness, and loss deep inside. And they are unable to recognize the emotional needs of others around them. They cannot identify with another person's feelings. Yet family relationships are, by nature, emotionally intimate. The only impact an emotionally disconnected man can have on his loved ones is a destructive one.

When a Man Focuses on Relationships with Women

A man may seek to soothe his deep wound through relationships with women. This will cause his marriage to suffer. A man's marriage cannot escape the destructive consequences of his emotional dependence upon women other than his wife. The suffering will also spill over to his children.

He may seek emotional bonds with women. Many men learned that they cannot share their hurts, fears, or worries with their fathers. Most men do not even consider other men as a possible source of comfort or support when they feel pain or face trouble. It is uncomfortable and depressing to face and grapple with the grief and emotional loss they feel inside. When men have suffered in their relationships with their fathers they turn to women to console their sorrow. They find it more comfortable to be understood and cared for by women. To develop close relationships with men is risky, frightening, and foreign.

A man may marry a woman because he feels that she understands and cares about him. She fills the deep emotional void he feels inside. But such a relationship carries tremendous risk. The truth is that no woman can ever fill a man's emotional need for connection with other men. A man who marries a woman because he feels understood and cared for by her puts unrealistic demands and impossible expectations upon her. Later in life, the man will realize that his wife has not met his needs or fulfilled his expectations. He may then turn to another woman who seems to understand or care for him better. He may go through life seeking woman after woman. He expects each one to meet a need that no woman can.

A man who does find healing through relationships with other men will often have poor boundaries with women. He may find it easier to talk with women. So when he has difficulty talking with his wife, he may share his frustrations and problems with another woman—a coworker or friend. This creates a problem. A man who develops a sharing relationship with a woman bonds with her. It is an emotional bond, and it is a violation of his marital boundaries. When this happens, his wife will often feel a loss or distancing in her relationship with her husband. This, of course, causes damage to the marriage.

Emotional bonding with another woman often sets the stage for an extramarital affair. And this opens the door for suffering and harm to his marriage and children. A man who is having an affair pours his time and emotional energy into the new relationship. His relationship with his children is left unattended. His children suffer feelings of abandonment and emotional distancing from their father. They may not even know he is having an affair, but they feel its effect.

His views of sexuality will be distorted. Men who seek healing relationships with women may have a distorted sexual image of women. They may also be drawn toward sex-love addiction. They may seek romance and sex as a way to fill the deep wound they feel inside. Both of these characteristics destroy a marital relationship.

An unrealistic expectation of a sexual relationship with a woman may drive a man to find the "perfect woman" to match his fantasy. This fantasy often comes from the way women are portrayed on television, in movies, and through pornography. In reality, he seeks a sexual goddess who is always sexually interested, sexually assertive, and sexually responsive. No woman on earth matches this fantasy. Yet this myth persists. It continues to injure marriages and harm relationships.

A man who lives under the illusion of this fantasy cannot be truly empathetic with his wife. He cannot comprehend the possibility that his wife may not always be interested in sex. He does not understand that his wife's sexual desire can be affected by other spiritual, emotional, or physical factors. The reality of his relationship with a real, human wife shatters his sexual fantasy. He may become angry. This anger further damages their relationship and leads to greater emotional distance between them.

A man with a sex-love addiction, has superficial or sexually-oriented relationships with women. If the primary bond in his relationship with his wife is sexual, the marriage will not last. The truth is, this type of man relates primarily to sexual excitement—not to the person with whom he has a sexual relationship. As time progresses, a woman who is the object of a sex-love addiction will feel used, abused, and manipulated. This kind of interaction is destructive to any intimate relationship between a man and a woman. It is particularly tragic in the marriage relationship.

A man obsessed with sexual fantasies develops a fundamental disrespect for women. This lack of respect may be evident in the sexual comments he makes about or to women. It is seen in the dirty jokes he tells. The man may also fantasize about the women he meets or sees. He visually undresses them with his eyes. Women notice these behaviors. They feel violated and unsafe. They usually distance themselves from these men.

A man who indulges in these fantasies betrays his wife. Inwardly, he is looking for greener pastures. He is hoping to find the perfect woman. Many men believe that their fantasies do not harm anyone. But there is a fine line between recreational fantasy, obsession, and acting on the fantasy. The Bible asks, "Can a man take fire in his bosom, and not be burned?"

Compulsive masturbation is a way some men fuel their fantasies. It becomes a means of relaxation and self-nurturing. These men will not seek relationships with other men who can help sort out these difficult issues. Instead, they may turn to sexually explicit television programs, magazines, videos, and websites as stimuli to perpetuate the fantasies. These actions may make a man feel better for a time, but they destroy the emotional bridge between a man and his wife. And these behaviors represent the breakdown of the man's spiritual relationship with God.

There is hope in healing. Doug is one man who depended on relationships with women to meet his emotional needs. He loved his wife and children, but he had no boundaries in his relationships with women. It was easy for him to share his problems and frustrations with women at work. Many times a woman at work would become his primary source of emotional support—then a sexual partner. His problem was made worse by frequent business trips for his company. Each city had at least one or two women with whom he would call and spent the night.

Life changed for Doug when his wife found out about one of his many affairs. She gave him a choice: counseling or divorce. Doug agreed to see a marriage counselor. The counselor recommended that Doug begin individual therapy as well. That is when he came to me.

It was apparent that Doug was sexually addicted. He could not even remember the number of women with whom he'd had sex. He was so involved with his addiction that he had not considered the possibility of contracting AIDS. He considered himself to be a Christian, yet he felt no guilt about betraying his wife or disobeying God. He was living two separate lives. He believed that his sexual behavior harmed no one, and therefore did not matter.

Whenever I counsel a man like Doug, who has a sex-love addiction, I suggest that he attend a twelve-step group for that addiction. I also encourage him to form his own support group of men. They need to be emotionally vulnerable and spiritually supportive of one another. And I strongly urge him to make a connection with his inner child. This allows him to become aware of his feelings.

Doug laughed at my suggestions. He did not believe it was possible for men to be supportive or understanding. In his mind women, not men, offered understanding, sympathy, and nurturing. He saw other men only as rivals and competition in the workplace. Doug also thought the idea of connecting with his inner child was silly. He went along with my suggestions—only because his marriage depended on his continued counseling.

In our sessions, I began to explore Doug's childhood. Doug had been raised primarily by his mother. He had few memories of his relationship with his father. As an adult, Doug had angry feelings when he was around his father. So he kept his distance from him. To get to the root of these memories, I asked Doug to close his eyes and picture himself as a young boy. An image of himself at seven years old came into his mind. I asked him what the little boy was feeling.

He gasped and said, "He feels pain on the back of his legs and lower back."

"What's happening to the little boy?" I asked.

Doug shook and cried out, "His father is hitting him with a belt. He's yelling and screaming at him. His father is telling him that he's a bad, bad boy. He says that he will never be anything good."

"What would you like to do to help that boy?" I asked.

"I want to tell his father that he has no right to hit his son like that. I want to tell him to get out of the room and stay out!"

"Let me know when you have done that for that hurt little boy." I said. Then Doug nodded his head. I continued, "Now take the little boy to a safe place where his father can't hurt him."

Doug took his seven-year-old little boy to a safe place surrounded by boulders and next to a mountain stream. I then asked, "How do you want to comfort that little boy?"

"I don't know if I can," Doug answered. "The little boy is afraid of men."

"Tell the little boy you understand," I suggested. "His father, the most significant man in his life, has hurt him badly. Tell the little boy that you and I understand why he doesn't trust men. Tell him that we feel sad because he had to suffer so much hurt."

Doug began to sob. "He wants me to hold him, but I have to be careful—his back and legs are bruised."

I encouraged Doug to picture a warm, beautiful beam of sunlight coming down from his Heavenly Father. I told him that the light could touch and heal the places where the little boy was wounded. I told him that it could melt away the bad things his father had said about him. I told him it was okay to hurt and to cry. I told him that God had made him in a special way. I told him that he could learn to become the man God intended him to be. Doug continued to cry and comfort the child he envisioned. It was healing for the child within.

The process of connecting with his inner child opened up Doug's memories. He began to heal the deep wounds he suffered from his father. He began to understand why he resisted supportive relationships with other men. He realized that his father had given him a strong message that men cannot be trusted.

Doug recognized that his mother had been his only safe parent. But his relationship with her was emotionally incestuous. She shared with him the frustration and anger she felt in her relationship to Doug's father. He began to remember how good it felt to be held by a girl in his early adolescence. He also recalled the times that his father had talked with him about the affairs he was having. He also remembered being sexually molested by a neighbor who paid him to perform oral sex.

These memories helped melt away his resistance to working a twelve-step program. Through his twelve-step work, he was able to feel the healthy guilt and shame of betraying his wife and disobeying God. The Christianity he had known in his head began to be felt in his heart. He began to heal.

Now, Doug's primary relationships are with men, and his boundaries with women are firm. He is alone with a woman only to conduct business. When he begins to desire her sexually, he contacts a supportive male friend to help him work through the crisis. If he is away from home overnight, he finds an *Overcomers Outreach* group or another twelve-step meeting to attend. Doug still has much to do to rebuild the emotional bridges to his wife and children; but he has found healing through a connection with his inner child and in relationships with men.

When a Man Can't Feel

A man who fills his emptiness through relationships with other women exposes his wife and children to the impact of his pain. Another way he may deal with inner pain is to distance or disconnect himself from that pain. Again, his family will feel the impact. His solution to the problem is disconnection from feelings. If he cannot feel emotions or understand the emotions of others, family intimacy is destroyed. A man, who has not come to grips with his inner feelings, may be unable to feel anything.

From a very early age, boys are taught to suppress their feelings. They learn that "big boys don't cry"—no matter what. They learn to deny whatever physical, emotional, or spiritual pain they feel. They learn that "real men" can conquer anything. Real men do not need to depend on help from others. They learn to feel no pain or fear. They learn to show no weakness. This creates great trouble for men and their families.

Men who don't feel emotionally don't feel physically. The impact of the "feel no pain— show no weakness" mentality is obvious at lunch time on Sundays. In almost every restaurant, groups of older women—widows—sit together. They enjoy the benefit of their dead husbands' hard work. Why is there an abundance of widows? Because in America, men usually live ten years less than women. Why do men die earlier? One reason is their denial of feelings.

The denial of emotional and physical pain go hand in hand. A man who is disconnected from what he feels emotionally tends to be disconnected from what he feels physically. As a result, men often ignore their aches and pains until they have major problems. Illnesses that could have been treated easily are ignored until they require major intervention. The first time many men seek regular medical care is after they have a major heart attack. What a sad result of not being in touch with one's feelings!

A man who is unaware of his feelings also has difficulty communicating with his wife and children. He finds it difficult to work through problems, respect his wife, and be sensitive to the emotional needs of those around him. He also tends to shame his wife and children.

Men who are disconnected emotionally have trouble relating to their families. A man must make some connection with his own hurt in his relationship with his father. Without that connection, he is incapable of feeling what others feel. And he cannot feel the emotional impact of his behavior on others.

For example, a father may be very angry. But he may not recognize that he feels that way. His wife and children certainly know he is angry! They may even try to tell him so. But he will reject their perceptions of his anger. He may say, "No, I'm not! I'll show you what real anger is!" Then display the fury of absolute rage. That's what he defines as anger.

What is happening in a situation like this? The father is unable to accept the reality of his family's perception. His perceptions are the only truth he will accept. It takes growth for a man to accept his family's perception of him regardless of how he feels about it. It takes even more maturity for a man to accept that word without the need to react to their feelings.

It is vitally important for a man to take a hard look at himself. Then he must respond to what he sees and to what his family sees. If his family perceives him as angry, they probably feel afraid of him, too. This fear damages their relationship with him.

Most men have not dealt with their own grief. So they cannot begin to understand, respect, or respond to another person's feelings. They do not have a clue as to what their families are trying to tell them. They are filled with their own shame and denial of feelings. Their only response is defensiveness and more anger.

I worked with a family that struggled with these things. Andy, the husband and father, could not believe that he was a controlling, angry man. His intense denial caused him to believe that his problems originated in his wife and children. Anyone close to him knew he was angry. He also carried a tremendous load of shame. He could not allow himself to acknowledge the truth about himself.

Andy's experience is not unusual. Men who have high levels of shame find it difficult to admit their wrongs. They believe they are really bad. Recovery can help men acknowledge their failure, reflect on it, make amends, and move on. But Andy stayed in denial with tragic results. Eventually his wife left him. She needed to find emotional safety for herself and their children.

Many men need to be in constant control of their families. When they cannot control them, anger results. This is a huge issue for men and not easily resolved. A man needs relationships with other men in order to identify and work through his feelings. Tom Watson, Jr., a father of six children, shares what it was like for him. He had to come to grips with his work-related feelings at IBM and his family:

> By the time I got home, there would be nothing left of me. I'd walk in and find the usual disorder of a large household— one of the kids had shot a BB gun at a passing car, or two of them were fighting, or somebody had bad grades. These things would strike me as crises that needed to be resolved right away, and yet I had no energy to bring to bear. I'd feel a desperate wish for somebody else to step in and make the decisions so I didn't have to. That's when I'd blow up. The kids would scatter like quail and Olive would catch the brunt of my frustration.... It took me years to grasp the fundamental difference between running a com-

pany and heading a family. IBM was like driving a car: when I came to a corner, I could steer around it very nicely, and off the car would go down a new road. I hit bumps here and there, but generally the car went where I wanted. With my family, this wasn't the case. The family was more like a car with two steering wheels, or multiple steering wheels, and only one of them belonged to me. I kept trying to exercise more control than I had.

When I saw I could not bend my wife and children to my will, I'd feel totally thwarted and boxed in. Those were the blackest moments of my adult life. An argument with Olive and the kids would sometimes make me so morose that the only thing I could do was hole up. I'd lock myself in my dressing room and Olive would stand on the other side of the door and try to get me to come out. Finally she'd reach the end of her rope. She'd call my brother and say, "Can't you come cheer Tom up?" Dick would come down from New Canaan. He always knew how to make my responsibilities seem lighter and draw me back into the world.[1]

How fortunate Tom Watson, Jr. was to have a man in his life who could help him deal with his feelings and bring him back to reality.

Men who are disconnected from their feelings will, without even trying, shame their children. Children have a deep emotional need to be listened to and understood. A father who does not respond to his child's feelings communicates that the child is unimportant. This lack of recognition and response causes the child to feel shame. Shame creates tremendous emotional damage. It makes children feel as if something about them is bad.

Remember, children need an emotional bond with their fathers. They need understanding and empathy. It is impossible for a father to identify with his children unless he understands some of his own feelings. I can see this in my own life. I have four children— two young adults and two at home. I have developed a deeper emotional connection with the younger children. When my older children were young, I was not in touch with my own anger, shame, and fear. So I wasn't as responsive as I can be now.

Let me share an example of the empathy I developed. Once, one of the younger children had a massive temper tantrum in Taco Bell. I tried everything I could think of to get her settled. (Yes, even therapists do not always know how to deal with their children!) At last, I took her out to the car and gave her one swat on the bottom. The spanking was more symbolic than actual. It caused no physical pain, but it had a tremendous impact on my daughter. In fact, two days later she approached me in the family room. She walked, quiet as a mouse and squeaked, "Daddy, somebody spilled Coke all over the entryway."

I had seen her bike and the can of Coke there earlier. So I suspected what had happened. I also saw the fear in her eyes and tension in her body. "Are you afraid you're going to get a spanking?" I asked.

She started to cry. I sat down, held her, and said, "I'm sorry. There is a big difference between what happened at Taco Bell and this accident. We'll clean this up together. It's no big deal." At once, she relaxed and the tears went away. I also learned and felt how devastating corporal punishment is. I wonder now if it is even an option.

I missed a lot of that kind of interaction when my older children were young. But it is never too late. Now when I overreact or become angry with them, it's easier to see the hurt in their eyes. I know that I need to reach out to them and respond differently. I have the chance to repair some of the damage that occurred in our day-to-day lives together. It was damage of which I was not even aware.

Men who are disconnected from their feelings often are unable to respect or care for their wives. The extent to which a man is connected to his feelings dramatically affects his marriage. The more a man feels, the more he can identify with and honor his wife's needs. The more a man is disconnected from his feelings, the less he is able to identify or care about his wife's desires. A man who is not in touch with his emotions will not notice how his wife feels. This is true of his wife's sexual and emotional needs. His wife may tell him that she has had a hard day. She may receive only a passing grunt in response. No wife feels respected in that kind of interaction.

This lack of respect also is seen in how a man responds to his wife's hopes and aspirations. A man who is not connected to his feelings is fearful of and unable to support his wife's personal development. His wife may want to pursue something important to her. She may want to go to college and earn a degree. She may want to go to work or assume a particular responsibility at church. She may want to have children. But an emotionally disconnected man may not have room for such changes in his life. He may not want to make the necessary adjustment for his wife's sake. He may sabotage her efforts, even if those activities would benefit her.

Robert Bly tells the story of a man who lacked both the respect and the ability to truly care for the woman he loved.

A long, long time ago, a young man would stand by his window at night, looking out at the starry sky. He would say to the stars, "I wish, I wish, that a beautiful woman would come to me, take care of me, and love me completely and deeply." This was his nightly ritual. Not a night went by that he did not make this wish to the stars.

One night, one of the stars that glowed so brightly came down into his room and became a beautiful woman. The young man looked at her, he desired her, and they made love all night long. When morning came, he looked at the woman and said, "What am I to do with you?"

"I don't know," she answered.

"I can't leave you alone here," the young man said.

"Someone might find you."

So he took a bottle with a stopper and asked the beautiful woman to go inside, which she did. He put the stopper in the bottle, tucked it into his pocket, and went about his business. That night when he came home, he opened the bottle to let the woman out, and they made love again all night long. In the morning, he returned her to her place in the bottle. He repeated this ritual for many, many days. Although he barely noticed, the woman's eyes became redder and redder with each passing day.

One morning, when the man let her out of the bottle, she said, "That is enough!" She then reached into her pocket, pulled out three seeds, and threw them down to the ground.

Immediately a giant tree shot up to the heavens. The woman began climbing up the tree, toward the starry heavens.

"Don't go!" the young man called after her. "Please don't leave me. I can't live without you."

She ignored his pleas and continued climbing upward, so he followed her.

"Don't follow me," she warned. "You cannot come with me.

It will be the death of you."

The young man ignored her words and continued to follow her, pleading and begging her to stay. But then he looked down and saw the ground far below him. Suddenly he fell and died.[2]

Women are no different from men in their need for personal growth. The man in the story only valued the woman sexually. He did not value her as a person. He did not regard her dreams, goals, and desires. Women with a desire or calling to do something need to do it. A man out of touch with his feelings will not understand the truth about his wife. He will not understand that her whole body and spirit will suffer if she cannot pursue her God-given desires and leading. Her suffering can lead to depression, illness, and even death. He does not realize that if he ignores his wife's feelings and needs, their relationship will not last.

On the other hand, a man who is emotionally connected will feel the value of his wife's personal development. He will support her even if it means making personal sacrifices. For example, I love to play basketball. If I could, I would still spend many evenings at the gym playing in some kind of league. In fact, I did for a number of years. But music is important to my wife Karen. She comes alive and feels a great sense of purpose and fulfillment when she is involved in church music. So every Wednesday night, from 4 p.m. on, the kids are my responsibility. And on Sunday mornings, it is my responsibility to get them ready for church. My commitment to the family at these times is necessary so that Karen can participate in choir and handbell activities. It is important that she knows I'll be there to take care of the family so she can pursue her interests.

I still play basketball and work out at a health club several times a week. My needs are not ignored. But I make sure that I do not prevent Karen's needs from being met. This is one way I am able to show her how deeply I care for her. I would not be able to do this if I were not in touch with my own feelings.

Men, who are not well connected with their feelings, lack a basic respect for women and children in general. They have a decreased sensitivity to the impact of their words and actions upon others. Many men today, 50 years old and older, have made lewd comments to the women they work with. They told off-color jokes. Such behavior is now considered to be sexual harassment. In fact, it has always been harassment. Many of these men are now in shock. They considered their actions to be normal and harmless. They never realized they were doing anything offensive.

Christian culture is not exempt from this lack of respect and care for women and children. Some accepted and traditional, Christian attitudes toward women are not truly biblical. Accepted practices that fail to recognize the value of women and to respect their role in church and family life are not godly. Some churches, for example, have overemphasized a wife's submission to her husband. They demand her submission in all circumstances even if the husband is abusive. This has fostered codependency among women and enabled some husbands to remain in their addictions.

Current attitudes toward abortion demonstrate the lack of emotional connection that men have. They are unable to feel the impact of their actions. In our society, abortion is viewed as an exclusively feminine issue. It is a feminine issue, of course. But it is also a masculine issue. Men participate in creation of each new life, yet many have little concern for that life. The lack of care for their unborn children reveals a great deal about men. There is something very sad about a father who is so selfish or out of touch with himself that he does not value the new life he has created.

A man changes when he becomes aware of his father-son wound. He begins to really feel what is inside. He becomes aware of the impact of his words. He is able to empathize and imagine the impact of those words. He is able to respect and care for his wife in ways he could not even imagine before. He is able to listen to the needs of his children. He is able to respond to them out of the fullness of his heart.

Men who are emotionally connected are also spiritually activated. They take steps to meet the needs they see and feel in church and family. Men who are in touch with their feelings have a deep and powerful concern for the new life they create. They become strong advocates for their children. They do everything they can to enable their children to develop into adulthood. By healing from their own woundedness, men are able to help heal the wounds of others.

A Closer Look

Sex-Love Addiction—All addiction grows from a person's desire to be in control. Rather than trust in God, we rely on our own devices and follow our own desires. The drug of choice, in this case sex-love, is used to meet an unmet need. It is used to distract or kill pain. It is used to take control and manipulate the circumstance of one's life. But the problem with addiction is actually the loss of control. The drug of choice becomes the master. The person becomes its slave. And every addiction carries its own curse—its own sorrow. The only solution to addiction is surrender. We must return control to the only One able to manage our lives. We must surrender to God and his will for our lives.

The Twelve-Steps—The following are the Twelve Steps of Alcoholics Anonymous. The word "alcohol" in Step One can be replaced with other issues or drugs of choice. For example, one might put "We admitted we were powerless over our broken past...."

1. We admitted we were powerless over alcohol—that our lives had become unmanageable.
2. Came to believe that a Power greater than ourselves could restore us to sanity.
3. Made a decision to turn our will and our lives over to the care of God as we understood Him.
4. Made a searching and fearless moral inventory of ourselves.
5. Admitted to God, to ourselves, and to another human being the exact nature of our wrongs.
6. Were entirely ready to have God remove all these defects of character.
7. Humbly asked Him to remove our shortcomings.
8. Made a list of all persons we had harmed, and became willing to make amends to them all.
9. Made direct amends to such people wherever possible, except when to do so would injure them or others.
10. Continued to take personal inventory and when we were wrong promptly admitted it.
11. Sought through prayer and meditation to improve our conscious contact with God as we understood Him, praying only for knowledge of His will for us and the power to carry that out.
12. Having had a spiritual awakening as the result of these steps, we tried to carry this message to alcoholics, and to practice these principles in all our affairs.

Reprinted with permission of Alcoholics Anonymous, World Services, Inc.

Twelve-Step Support Groups—A variety of support groups have grown to embrace the healing power of the twelve-steps. The power of the steps is the power of God as we know him in Jesus Christ. The spirituality of the steps is the power of the truth. As we face our lives, feel our pain, acknowledge our wrongs, take responsibility, and surrender to the will of

God, we come into a proper relationship to truth. And Jesus said, "The truth shall set you free!"

Recovery—Recovery is the journey toward healing that begins when we recognize that our lives are broken and beyond our ability to mend. The form that recovery takes will vary according to the individual—twelve steps, psychotherapy, spiritual experience, mind and body healing, etc. In some cases, recovery begins in our late 30s and 40s because unconscious physical and psychological processes urge us to seek health and a greater well-being. By this time, our well-practiced coping strategies don't work as they once did. The pain of destructive relationships or life-style patterns intensifies and cries out for resolution. The physical impact of internal pain and tension begins to appear through illness or disease. Psychological and spiritual decay leads to physical breakdown. When the physical signs appear, we have a choice to make. We can continue in our denial and ignore the signs, or we can face the difficulties head on. In some cases, we are forced to make that choice—physical conditions threaten our life. The move toward spiritual and emotional healing moves us toward physical healing as well. And the journey toward healing brings out our core self. The recovery process uncovers the true person inside. It releases gifts and unique potential.

Personal Reflection

1. Describe a situation in your life when you were *overly* dependent upon a woman for your emotional needs.

2. In what ways do you relate to being emotionally numb—out of touch with your feelings?

3. Describe how you have been disrespectful of women in the past. Do you currently have attitudes about women that you believe are harmful?

4. Have you ever believed that you were "addicted" to a person, substance, or behavior? Explain.

5. What is your personal recovery experience? How do you relate to the description of recovery above?

NOTES:

CHAPTER 5

The Father-Son Wound and a Man's Career

A son instinctively feels a sense of loss when he has no emotional connection with his father. Still, he may not be able to recognize or identify what he has missed. He experiences loss in their relationship, but he also feels the loss in his masculine identity. The emotional bridge between father and son touches the heart of the son's masculine soul. The son with no bridge to his father misses his identity as a son and as a man. So as a boy grows into manhood, he devotes much of his energy toward building an emotional bridge to his father.

A man's work is an important part of his life. Our culture tends to view it as the most important part. A man often uses his career to bridge the emotional gap between himself and his father. Natural ability, training, and opportunity play key roles in a man's career. But the father wound is also a dominant and driving force. A man can become addicted to work. He can allow his work to replace his family relationships. He can be easily manipulated by his employers. He can be driven to achieve the impossible. Or he may have trouble getting or keeping a job. He may feel unworthy and work himself into an early grave. All this to prove his worth to his dad. These possibilities, and many more, relate directly to a man's relationship with his father.

Approval Through Achievement

A son may try to reach his father through achievement. Tom

Watson, Jr. is a prime example of a son who hungered for an emotional bond with his father. Like many sons, he tried to earn his father's recognition and acceptance through remarkable achievements. He guided and grew IBM, the company his father founded, into a mammoth, worldwide corporation. In the late 1940s, a few years after he took over management of IBM, he doubled the company's gross sales from $70 million to $140 million. All the time, he longed for his father to notice his accomplishments. He hungered for a clear and direct acknowledgment of his success and an affirmation that his father accepted him as both a man and a businessman.

That affirmation did not come easily. The elder Watson trusted his son in some areas of the business, but considered him to be totally incompetent in other areas. And he was not afraid to tell him so. After one heated discussion, the younger Watson received a note from his father that said:

> 100%
> Confidence
> Appreciation
> Admiration
> Love
> Dad[1]

Not long after that, his father formally passed the leadership of IBM to his son.

For many men, the drive to gain their fathers' approval begins at an early age. Young boys often seek their fathers' approval through the sports their fathers love. The struggle for acceptance is apparent at any youth league for baseball, basketball, soccer, or football. It's easy to spot the boy who scans the crowd in search of dad. His disappointment is clear. The loss is plain to see—his father is not there. Perhaps work kept him away. Maybe alcohol is the problem. Or a woman other than the boy's mother occupies his father's attention.

There are others like the boy who works hard, yet he lacks the skills to be on the field. He warms the bench. He longs to hear his father cheer for him. But instead, he bites his lip as his father cheers for teammates on the field. It's clear to everyone that he's not the best. Oh sure, he's a part of the team, but he wants more. He wants praise and recognition from the one who matters—his father.

There was a boy like this on my son's soccer team. The boy was a joy to watch. He was a natural sprinter. He ran like the wind and controlled the ball, too. The other team knew his potential. When he got the ball, it became a one-on-one challenge between him and the goalie. And that the goalie usually lost.

During one game, my son's team was winning—everyone had played well. His star teammate broke through and headed toward the goal. This time something changed. Instead of a direct run at the goalie, the star player passed the ball. He kicked it to a teammate who scored. He allowed the other boy the joy of the goal. It was a beautiful example of teamwork and sharing. The young speedster headed to the sidelines and was met by his father. The man was furious. He ridiculed his son for not taking the goal for himself. Throughout the season, that boy's father never enjoyed his son's accomplishments. The boy ran and played as hard as he could, but he would forfeit the acceptance and affirmation he so desired. His father never patted his back or put his arm around him. He never said, "Great job!" or "I'm proud of you, son."

A boy does not lose the intense desire to prove himself to his father just because he becomes an adult. The little boy is still waiting. His need was never met. An inward motivation drives the man to succeed. The young man looks to bosses and supervisors for the approval he still desires from his father. The son may not be aware of his need for affirmation until he faces some kind of crisis.

A young man's drive for achievement may have a variety of results. Some men esteem success in their career more than a personal investment in their families. A man may be so intent on climbing the corporate ladder that he accepts any transfers his company requests. He may give little or no thought about the impact of a move upon his family. Another man may be so intent to gain approval that he will attend an unscheduled work meeting and miss his son's birthday party. Many men become addicted to work in their search for fatherly approval.

Work Addiction

A man who yearns for his father's approval can fall into the trap of overworking. Overwork brings approval from employers and supervisors. Coworkers may even appear to respect his long hours. Success at work makes a man feel important. It makes him feel good enough to ignore some of the pain he feels inside. These good feelings cause a man to devote even more hours and energy to his work.

But those good feelings are based on performance only. Away from the workplace, he loses them. Work becomes an emotional "fix" for him. That is why some men become depressed and even die within a few years of retirement. They base their sense of self-worth on their success in the workplace. When their basis for self-worth is removed, they see no reason to continue life.

Work addiction also has physiological side effects. A man involved in overwork and compulsive activity experiences a consistent level of excitement and intensity. It is difficult to achieve this apart from work. His intensity at work causes an adrenaline high. An adrenaline addiction results. Even a major crisis provides an exciting diversion for him. If his work intensity declines, he will feel fatigued and depressed. He experiences adrenal letdown or withdrawal. They are the same feelings that occur with withdrawal from alcohol or drugs.

Men who succumb to the psychological and physiological effects of work addiction have room for little else in their lives. They work long hours and do not notice that their lives are being spent away from their families. To a work-addicted man, a 40 hour week feels like a part-time job—even a 60 hour week seems short. Friendships for a work-addicted man are usually superficial. And his relationships are work-centered. The work-addicted man is mentally and emotionally obsessed with the next task on his list. He has little, if any, awareness of who he is or how he feels inside. He may be oblivious to the events around him.

Tom, a client of mine, is a classic example of work addiction in action. One day, he was in his normal rush to an appointment. He drove in busy traffic, directed workers via cell phone, and communicated with men in his warehouse via two-way radio. He turned to scratch notes on a pad of paper and slammed into the car ahead of him! The driver of the other car came back to talk with him, but Tom had to finish his phone call. Without dropping a beat, Tom called a tow truck and also arranged for a rental car. Tom continued work in the tow truck. The rental car awaited him at the body shop. He jumped into the driver's seat and continued his day.

The accident caused thousands of dollars of damage, but inconvenienced Tom for less than an hour. He continued to juggle all the balls and keep his company going. The adrenaline rush of the accident was business-as-usual for Tom. It was just a ripple in crisis routine. Only a work addict can operate this way. The addiction takes a tremendous toll on his life and family. For some men, work even replaces their family relationships.

Replacing Family Relationships with Work

The family nature of some work relationships can be positive. An older man who mentors a young man serves as a guide. A younger man needs that kind of support as he develops in his profession. Samuel Osherson has extensively studied how a man's life is shaped by his relationship with his father. He says, "A powerful mentor may speak to the hunger vulnerable young men have for a strong, all-accepting father-hero, whom we can love and revere unambivalently.... For many young men, mentors truly become the better fathers they yearn for."[2]

The mentor (or supervisors, managers, or peers) provides camaraderie, affirmation, and value for the younger man. These elements are vital for a man's continued development. They are often the very things missing from the man's relationship with his father. Yet even these good relationships have a toxic side.

Consider Jim, who was assigned a mentor when he first joined a major computer company. The older man had been with the company for years and was highly skilled in his particular area. His job was to educate Jim about the company and its policies. He was supposed to help him successfully navigate within the organization. A warm, supportive relationship developed between the two. Jim felt comfortable enough to share some personal struggles with him. He talked about the difficulty of the move for his family—the

new area and all. He also shared his fear that he would not succeed. The mentor assured Jim of his continued support during this
period of adjustment. He recognized Jim's skills and encouraged
him to continue to develop his potential.

Jim was touched by his mentor's concern and encouraged by
their relationship. The needs of the little boy within him began to
be met. The parts of Jim that had been untouched by his own father
were quickened. Hungry for nourishment, Jim became like a little
boy anxious to please his dad. He began to overwork. He was ea-
ger to go to work and go the extra mile at work to please this older
man. It became harder and harder for him to leave work and go
home to his family. His deepest emotional needs were being met on
the job.

Jim's situation is not all that unique. When a man's emotional
needs are met through work, it is easy for work and work relationships to take the place of his family. On the job, people give him
praise and encouragement for his great work and extra effort. He
may receive more affirmation from his secretary than he ever received from his wife. Of course, his wife might affirm him more if
he spent more time with her! If his primary emotional needs are
being met at work, chances are good that some work addiction
exists. And it makes work more appealing than family.

When the work-addicted man finally comes home, his family
may not be that happy to see him. Undercurrents of distrust, anger,
resentment, and abandonment may poison the air. They have been
hurt because he has been away so much. Before long he may get
into a fight with his wife or kids and say, "Enough of this!" To
escape, he retreats back to the office. At work he does not have to
face such conflicts or discomfort. If you asked this man if his family is important to him, he would say, "Yes! Of course my family is
important. Look how hard I work for them. Look what I buy for
them. They have nice cars, good educations, and a financially secure future." But his children miss what they need most—their
father. They would much rather have his heart, his spirit, his time,
and his physical presence.

It is great when some of a man's emotional needs are met
through his work. And it is a great tragedy when a man allows his
work to replace his family in his heart. It is a man's deep emotional

needs that propel him to replace his family relationships with work and work relationships. He needs to find new ways to meet those needs. He needs to form close, committed relationships with other men. He must meet the deep unmet needs from his relationship with his father. He must fulfill them in ways that will not destroy him or his family.

Codependency and Chronic Overwork

Another approval-related consequence of the father-son wound is codependency. Like the work-addicted man, a codependent also uses his work as a way of proving his worth. But his method is a bit different. He may get so caught up in seeking approval from everyone at work, especially his boss, that he does not set good boundaries. He gets so focused on being loyal to the company that he cannot set limits on how much he works. He is not sure when the day should begin or end. He finds himself in a constant state of over-commitment and overwork. He becomes unable to say, "No!" He will try to do more than is humanly possible.

The codependent man is driven by the hope that he will receive acceptance, approval, and advancement. He seeks reward for his loyalty. The codependent man is unable to accurately assess what he is getting from the company in return for his labor. He is so caught up in seeking approval and pleasing others that he does not watch out for his own welfare. He may work for years and pay no attention to what he earns. He may never be able to meet his future financial needs. He may labor hard and long for a promotion that never comes. He may never realize that only the owner's family or employees with a certain college degree ever get advanced.

Ron was an example of a codependent man. His family was active in their church, but his father was an alcoholic. Ron was nine years old when his mother discovered that her husband was having an affair. Once the adultery was exposed, Ron's father left the family. He simply dropped out of Ron's life with no explanation. In reality, Ron's father had emotionally abandoned his family years earlier. His interests were consumed by alcohol and work.

Ron does not remembers feeling close to his dad. He does

remember that his mother was angry and humiliated by what happened. She stopped going to church and insisted that her children do the same.

As time passed, Ron buried his feelings of abandonment and shame. He hid them under a load of hard work and accomplishments. After college graduation, his diligence paid off. He landed a good job with a family-owned company. Ron joined that company and felt like he was part of the family. The little boy within him viewed the owner of the company as the father he never had. Through hard work and loyalty, Ron advanced quickly in the company. Soon he was in a position second only to the owner.

But there was a downside to Ron's apparent success and happiness. The little boy within him drove him to outperform himself to please his employer. His need for acceptance and approval blinded him to the owner's manipulation and control. He could believe nothing but good about his boss despite evidence to the contrary.

For example, Ron's boss offered him three weeks of vacation if he brought in an additional 15 percent in sales during the quarter. Ron would do whatever it took to achieve the goal. But when it was time to get his reward, his boss withdrew the carrot. "Cash flow is down," he would say. "I can't spare you just yet. Can you wait until next month to take the time off?" Ron could not bring himself to disappoint the owner. So instead he put off the vacation and disappointed himself. He felt more needed, valued, and important when his boss asked him to make sacrifices.

Ron seemed content to live this way. Over and over his boss held out a prize and then pulled it back when Ron accomplished the task. The toxic nature of this relationship with the owner began to take a heavy toll on Ron's life. His health started to deteriorate, and his wife threatened to leave him. That when he began counseling.

Ron was baffled with himself and asked, "How can I think so clearly and make such wise business decisions, yet give in when I face the boss?" He began to recognize the real issue when he asked for a Friday off. He wanted to go on a Boy Scout camping trip with his son. He had just put in an 80 hour week and had landed a major new contract. He opened up entirely new avenues of business and income for the company. Still, Ron's boss refused to give him a day off, and Ron missed an important time with his son.

The sadness in his son's eyes opened Ron's eyes. He realized that he had disappointed his son in this way many times before. For the first time, Ron began to feel some of that sadness. He understood his need to set boundaries with his boss. He decided to seek additional counseling and began attending a Codependents Anonymous group.

In recovery, Ron realized how the wounds of his father-son relationship had caused him to be out of control in his relationship with his boss. With the help of his sponsor, Ron began writing down how he would set boundaries with his boss. He set those boundaries and cut back on his work time. Ron realized that his codependence had allowed his boss to ignore Ron's need for an assistant. Ron was literally doing the work of two or three people!

As expected, the boss did not like it when Ron started to recognize his own needs and set boundaries. He became critical and angry. One day he even threatened Ron, "Either you work to meet the needs of this company as you did before, or you'll lose your job!" In the past, these words would have devastated Ron. The words were still frightening to hear, but now he had support and insight. He talked it over with his sponsor, his counselor, and his men's group. Armed with their perspective and support, Ron went to his boss and reaffirmed the boundaries he had set. He explained that he was no longer willing to work the long hours he had before. He explained that he needed at least one more person in his department in order to accomplish his work effectively. He also reminded his boss that he was a highly skilled and valuable employee. He ended by saying, "But if you still want to fire me, I have no problem with that."

Ron did not lose his job. In fact, he was able to hire the additional employees he needed, and he maintained his boundaries. Continued healing and growth moved Ron to consider starting his own business. The dysfunction and stress of his present company grew tiresome. And his own company would allow him to practice the values and attitudes he believed would lead to success.

Many men have struggled with codependent efforts to gain approval in the workplace. I see a bit of codependence in David when Saul offered him his daughter, Michal, in marriage. David did not feel worthy of such a great reward. So Saul demanded nothing less than 100 Philistine foreskins as the price for his daughter. David did not even consider that Saul named that price because he hoped David would die in the effort. Anxious to feel worthy, David went out and brought back not 100, but 200 foreskins! (See 1 Samuel 18:20-27).

The codependence that affected Ron in the workplace also affects some men in Christian service. Some missionaries, for example, have devoted their working years to service on foreign mission fields. Dedicated to the Lord and the organizations they serve, some of these men have never discussed their retirement needs with their mission board. They gave years of service under the assumption that the mission organization would take care of them in retirement. Not until they return home to retire do they realize that they have no resources on which to live.

Pastors, too, must deal with this issue. A recent survey of pastors indicated that 90 percent of them work more than 46 hours a week. A frightening 80 percent of them also believe their ministry adversely affects their families. And 70 percent of pastors say they do not have anyone they would consider to be a close friend.[3]

It is good that some men are willing to devote their lives to Christian service. However, a man who "serves the Lord" but harms himself or his family may have the wrong motivation. He may be serving out of a need to earn recognition and approval from his earthly father rather than out of his commitment to his heavenly Father. I encourage Christian men who desire to serve their heavenly Father to feel their grief and deal with the wounds in their relationships with their earthly fathers. Then they will be set free to truly serve God.

Unrealistic Expectations

A man's expectations for his career and success are affected by the kind of relationship he has with his father. Throughout every stage of life a man needs relationships with older men who will initiate him, support him, guide him, train him, and bring him along through the challenges of life. Life is never as easy, rewarding, or idyllic as a boy dreams it will be. Part of a father's responsibility is to help his son face the harsh reality of life.

I introduced my son, Ben, to some of life's harder truths. One of Ben's earliest jobs was to deliver realtors' brochures house-to-house. Once a month he deliver two thousand brochures. He was paid a nickel each. As he began this venture, I talked to him about the reality of business and the need to set aside some profit to cover overhead. I explained that since he carried the brochures in his backpack, that was his overhead. I also pointed out that his backpack was starting to fall apart. He would need to set aside some money to buy another one.

At the time he ignored me. But a few months later, he had more brochures to deliver, and his backpack was torn. He explained how hard it would be to carry the brochures by hand rather than in his pack. Then he asked if he could borrow some money for a new backpack. It was hard, but I said, "No. I will not lend you the money."

Was he upset with me! When he got paid, he went out and bought an expensive leather backpack. I knew he bought an expensive one out of anger. When he showed it to me I said, "That's a nice backpack, Ben. I'll bet it was expensive. But it's your money. You'll just have less to spend on other things you enjoy. And this one will wear out, just like the nylon ones do." A day later, Ben exchanged the leather backpack for a less expensive one. He was pleased to have twenty dollars left over.

This incident taught Ben several important principles. He learned that it is important to anticipate needs and plan for the future. He learned not to count on someone to bail him out. He also learned that if he did not have the money he needed, he would have to make do with what he had. And he learned to think carefully before making a purchase. In a small way this illustrates how a father can help his son deal with the realities of life.

The father's objective in providing reality checks for his son is not to kill his child's dreams. He must help him learn to make the right decisions in pursuing those dreams. When Ben grew older, he wanted a Toyota four-wheel-drive pickup truck. I agreed that it was a nice thing to have. When he looked in the newspaper and told me how expensive they were, I said, "These are hard decisions to make. People sometimes buy expensive things and have to spend all their time working to pay for those things. Sometimes it means giving up other things that are also important." Then I gave him our insurance agent's phone number. I told him to find out what the insurance would cost. (I could have told him how much it was, but in his mind my information would have seemed inaccurate or an exaggeration!) After he called the agent, he came back to me and said, "Dad! Do you know how much that insurance costs?"

"Yeah," I said, "It's a bummer, isn't it?"

This kind of input from the father or other men is essential to a young man growing into adulthood. Without it, a young man may grow up with a very unrealistic idea of who he is and what he is able to do. He may become a perpetual student who is great at acquiring knowledge but unable to take risks and turn that knowledge into a successful career. He may become a man who forever changes jobs. Moving from job to job, he may never be satisfied for more than a few months. He may get bored with what he is doing or the people with whom he works. He may be fired repeatedly and forced to change jobs because he does not have what it takes to do a job well over the long term.

Alan, a man in his 40, is an example of a man who missed out on the guidance and accountability a father can provide. He was deeply wounded by his father's death when he was just nine years old. Alan is brilliant. He reads widely and can carry on an intelligent conversation on almost any subject. He has taken all kinds of courses and amassed impressive credits, but he has never been successful in his career. He does not have a usable degree, nor can he keep a job for more than a few months. He is always months behind on his bills and has never been able to support his family.

What is his problem? It is not lack of ability; he can sell, invent, and design. It is not that he cannot get a job. In fact, people love him for the first month. After that they learn to hate him. He becomes arrogant, self-centered, sloppy, and does not follow through on his assignments. People soon learn that they cannot count on him, so he is turned out on the street—again.

This pattern goes back to the wound he suffered when his father died. When that happened, no other man—no grandfather, uncle, or man in the church—stepped forward to be there for him. No man was there to help him deal with his loss or to nurture and guide his fantastic intellect into a productive path. No man was there to make him accountable in dealing with life. When Alan reached late adolescence no man was there to say, "I will support you emotionally and teach you what I can, but you need to be responsible enough to pay your bills on your own."

Alan, who had several older female relatives, turned toward women to meet his needs. These relatives felt sorry for him and gave him money to bail him out. So he has never learned to be responsible or productive in his career.

When sons are not nurtured by their fathers through the early stages of life, they do not have a realistic picture of what it takes to be successful. Deep inside, many young men are looking for someone to say, "You're the greatest. You're wonderful!" They expect to start out making $75,000 a year. They have no idea that it may take years of low-paying, unfulfilling, menial, tedious work to achieve their ultimate career goals. They have little or no tolerance for jobs that are not what they ultimately want. So they end up frustrated, angry, and depressed at the realities of life.

Fathers play an incredibly important role in helping their sons develop successful, rewarding, and well-balanced careers. The wound in a man's relationship with his father greatly hinders his ability to meet his career goals. The father-son wound may drive a man to work addiction. It may cause him to be outwardly successful but inwardly destructive. It may cause him to imprison himself in a difficult and unrewarding career. It can even lead a man to fail to develop a career at all. When a man deals with his deep woundedness, however, he can begin to make real choices and real progress in his career.

A Closer Look

Work Addiction—A man, who yearns for his father's approval, can fall into the trap of overworking. Overwork brings approval from employers, supervisors, and coworkers. Success at work makes a man feel important. It makes him feel good enough to ignore some of the pain he feels inside. These good feelings cause a man to devote even more hours and energy to his work. Work becomes an emotional "fix" for him. A man involved in overwork and compulsive activity experiences a consistent level of excitement and intensity. His intensity at work causes an adrenaline high. An adrenaline addiction results. If his work intensity declines, he will feel fatigued and depressed. He experiences adrenal letdown or withdrawal. They are the same feelings that occur with withdrawals from alcohol or drugs.

Codependency—Caretaking, people pleasing, and unhealthy servitude or loyalty can be codependent behaviors. Codependency is an addiction to others, and it can take many forms. Some codependents help and "do" for others so that they can feel good about themselves. Their sense of self-worth comes from the value that others place upon them. They might work long hours and sacrifice themselves all for recognition or praise from the boss or the "biggies." Others enmesh themselves in the lives of others through controlling, fixing, or enabling. They mistake the dependence and neediness of others for love and commitment. Codependents live their lives through the experience of others. But it takes its toll. Codependents are often resentful, angry, tired, and worn. They are the martyrs. Their thankless efforts never scratch their deepest itch—all the concern for others leaves them bankrupt, empty, and ill.

Boundaries—Boundaries are the beliefs and feelings that serve as barriers to anything that might harm a person. They are essential to ensure the inner safety of every human being. They are like invisible fences that provide spiritual, emotional, and physical protection. I use the illustration of the medieval castle. The wall and the watchful sentries are a formidable obstacle to any attack. Boundaries enable us to know when we are at risk, and they give us the ability to take steps to protect ourselves. Boundaries help us define areas of personal responsibility and enable us to refuse responsibilities that belong to others. They keep toxic feelings and information out, and they provide the separation needed for healing to occur when we have been wounded.

Castle walls are made of stone. Fences are made of wire and wood. But what material are used to build boundaries? We use truth. Truth will set us free and keep us safe. For example, when another person rages at us, we embrace the truth. We speak truth to ourselves and to others. To myself I might think the following:

> *This person's rage is not about me. This unfortunate conduct is his problem. I am not responsible for it.*

> *I don't have to subject myself to this kind of abuse. I am free to remove myself from this situation.*

To the other person I might say the following:

I don't appreciate the way you are talking to me. If you want to discuss this or anything else with me, you must control your anger.

I deserve to be treated with respect and spoken to in a reasonable manner.

Personal Reflection

1. What work-related addictions or harmful patterns can you identify in your own life?

2. In what ways have you allowed your work-related problems to affect or harm your family?

3. Can you identify any codependent behavior in your work experience? In what ways have you sought the approval and acceptance of employers?

4. What boundaries do you use to protect yourself in your current work environment? Are they effective?

5. What unrealistic expectations have you had to work through in your work experience? Did you have any older man to help you face the realities of the real world?

NOTES:

CHAPTER 6

The Father-Son Wound and a Man's Spiritual Life

A man's relationship with his father impacts his spiritual life. The emotional detachment men learn from their fathers inhibits their spiritual development. And a man's personal relationship with God often mimics his relationship with his father.

Most men tend to be spiritually passive and inactive. They may go to church, but they are not really there. They may hear a sermon, but its message may not penetrate their hearts or make a difference in their lives. They may serve as ushers and greet others, but they may not connect with God. They may sit on the elder board and make decisions for the church, but they may not be able to commit heart and soul to the Lord.

A Growing Spiritual Vacuum

Men dominate pastoral staffs in most churches. Still, a masculine vacuum exists within local congregations. Many men attend services, but they tend to stay on the fringe of involvement. Many men lack the heart or passion to minister to others. The most disciplined men may read Scripture daily. Some may engage in factual discussions about the Bible. But few men feel the emotion, intensity, and spiritual impact of what Scripture reveals about God. Few can sense God's heart for mankind.

The lack of emotional connection with God causes most men to feel inadequate as spiritual leaders. They know that they need to meet God on a feeling level. Yet they do not know how. As a result, they feel shame and they withdraw from church. And the next generation is left with even less male leadership.

Consider how few men teach Sunday school. In most churches, a boy can attend Sunday school from infancy through high school and never have a male teacher. There too few male leaders (other than pastoral staff) who lead Bible studies or initiate church programs for men. In most churches, women either design or run a high percentage of church programs.

Today's Christian church is primarily a feminine church. I harbor no antifeminine feelings. Thank God for the women who are involved. Still, I grieve the vacuum left by the absence of men. I cannot help but wonder, *Where are the men? Where are the men who are spiritually alive? Where are the men who are full of passion and fire for God? Where are the men who hunger to grow in fellowship with God and other men? Where are the men who take bold risks in their faith? Where are the men who act in faith and share the gospel of Christ? Where are the men who reach out in love to their community beyond the church?*

The church needs strong, spiritual, and committed men. But they are difficult to find. Over the years, the lack of male leadership has stunted the church. The absence of male models and spiritually mature, older men has wounded the church. Men should serve as spiritual leaders—instead they feel shame for their lack. Men should assume the roles of teacher and model—instead they look to others. Many men chose to abandon the church (physically or emotionally) rather than deal with these feelings of shame and inadequacy.

Spiritual Expectations that Shame

Our traditional expectations of a man's spiritual leadership can produce shame. No one would pick a man out of the crowd and put him in an operating room with a patient. No one could expect just any man from the street to perform triple bypass surgery. Education, training, and supervised experience is required. But in the church, there is an unspoken expectation that every man ought to be a spiritual leader. This expectation is not realistic, nor is it fair.

Many men feel like they must be biblical scholars before they can open their mouths at church. They feel they have nothing significant to offer. This fear of failing to meet expectations keeps men on the outside of church life and ministry. It reinforces the masculine vacuum that exists. For instance, a man may be afraid to teach a Sunday school class for boys because he thinks he must teach deep theological truths. He may not realize that the real challenge is to contain all that youthful energy in one room for an hour! Of course, a man needs some knowledge of Scripture. He needs to prepare his lesson. But he does not have to be a great Bible scholar to teach a group of boys. The effective teacher knows how to connect with the boys. He shares from his heart what he has learned about God. And he uses Scripture and his own life experiences as his tools.

Any man—regardless of skills—can have an active ministry through the church. It is hard for men to realize that. A willing heart is all a man needs. Consider Bob. He felt a little ashamed because he had a construction trade, not a college education. Many in his church valued advanced, academic degrees. Folks often talked about what college they and their kids attended. Bob felt that he had little to talk about with them. No one seemed to value the kinds of trade skills he had.

Bob's attitude began to change after he spent some time with an uncle. He grew to value himself and appreciate what he had to offer others in his church. His uncle was a skilled carpenter and builder. He often told Bob how his talent and trade had come from his father—Bob's grandfather. These talks gave Bob a sense of pride. He came from several generations of builders. They were men who contributed a practical and substantial legacy to their community. Bob became more confident at church—more involved with other men. He expressed himself more often and made friendships.

Some of the men asked him to teach them a few basic, woodworking skills. He agreed and asked the men to bring their teenage sons. The lessons were full of fellowship and fun. Fathers and sons learned about woodworking side by side. An older man, with a skill and a desire to share, found fulfillment and joy. Bob was able to bring fathers and sons together in a special way. He created an experience for others that he never had with his father.

Teenagers continue to visit Bob's shop. He shares his time and heart with them. His emotional depth and spiritual growth rubs off. The boys gain a stronger image of what Christian manhood is all about. And because of Bob, they will grow in their understanding of God.

This is just one example of how a man can have an important and active spiritual involvement in the Christian community. A man's spiritual leadership in the home and church involves far more than his ability to teach or preach the Bible. A man can share his expertise and experiences in a wide variety of ways. A man, who cares enough to share his life with another man or boy, meets an important need in others. This connection teaches what it means to be a Christian man. It helps us better understand what it means to be loved by God.

A man does not become a mature Christian at the moment of his conversion. Nor does he become a godly person on his own. He develops character through contact with his father and other godly men. They model the spiritual life and leadership through everyday living. When his father and other men are not spiritually alive and active in the church, a man is left wounded and wanting.

Like many men of my generation and of generations before me, I have felt this woundedness. No men actively participated in my spiritual life as I grew up. My Sunday school teachers were women. I am thankful for the role they played in my spiritual development. I am thankful that they answered my questions and taught me the importance of Bible study and prayer. But the absence of men in my spiritual growth taught me that church was women's work. It taught me that church was less important than work and business. It taught me that normal men are passive and distant in relationship to God and his Church. But what I learned about masculine, Christian spirituality was and is wrong.

Emotionally Detached—Spiritually Detached

The spiritual life of many men goes no deeper than sitting in a pew on Sunday. They may thumb through the Bible and sing a hymn or two. Few of the spiritual principles are carried over into a man's daily life. I believe that a man's emotional detachment from the world around him contributes to an empty and fruitless spiritual life. A man numbed to his emotions is also numbed to spiritual feelings. He can know in his head that God loves him. But he must experience what it *feels* like to be loved by another person. Without the emotional experience of love, it is impossible to feel God's love. And it is impossible to live a life that is directed by that love.

Patrick Arnold, who wrote about the masculine spirituality in the Bible, expresses the problem of emotional and spiritual detachment this way:

> "I hurt inside as I see the great divorce that has developed over the generations between men and Christian spirituality. I hurt for the men that have lost the close contact with God that a healthy religiosity can nurture. This is an alienation that affects me personally as well as most men."[1]

Solomon is a good example of an emotionally and spiritually detached man. His life illustrates the divorce between spiritual knowledge and spiritual living. Solomon was filled with God's wisdom. He had been taught about God, and he had two personal encounters with Him (see 1 Kings 11:9). But I wonder how much of what Solomon experienced touched him on a feeling level. There is evidence of emotional detachment throughout his life. Scripture indicates that Solomon relied on a number of ways to numb his feelings:

▶alcoholism (see Proverbs 23:29-35),
▶compulsive work (Ecclesiastes 2:4-6),
▶compulsive spending (Ecclesiastes 2:7-8),
▶compulsive study (1 Kings 4:2~34),
▶compulsive sexual activity (1 Kings 11:3).

Solomon's writings, which include 3,000 proverbs and more than a thousand songs (1 Kings 4:32), also illustrate his spiritual detachment. These writings show a broad knowledge of God but little evidence of a deep, feeling relationship with God. Compare Solomon's proverbs with David's psalms. Solomon's proverbs convey spiritual knowledge but lack the passion, vitality, and personal relationship with God that David's psalms possess. The only evidence of an intimate, passionate relationship with God is in Solomon's prayer at the dedication of the temple (1 Kings 8:15-61).

The tragedy of Solomon's life is that he could not maintain his spiritual commitment to God. His personal encounters with God, his gift of wisdom from God, and his leadership position over God's holy nation could not keep him spiritually connected. By the end of his life, Solomon had lost touch with God. And his detachment from God had a devastating impact on his sons and the nation of Israel.

What was the source of Solomon's tragic emotional detachment? I believe it can be traced, at least in part, to his relationship with his father David. While king of Israel, David experienced a certain amount of emotional detachment from his family. For example, the rape of his daughter Tamar by her half-brother Amnon. He had feelings, but he was not moved enough to take action. This emotional detachment is what he modeled to his son Solomon. David's extramarital affair also wounded Solomon. David modeled that it was preferable to turn to women as a source of comfort and support rather than to men. Solomon's choices in life indicate the deep wounds he experienced in his heart.

The father-son wound continues to impact the spiritual lives of men today just as it did in Solomon's time. Dramatic and grand spiritual experiences were not enough to keep Solomon connected with God. To maintain godly Christian living for a lifetime, a man needs more. Spiritual truth must touch a man at the depths of his heart. But most men cannot experience that touch until they feel the pain of their wounded hearts and reach out for healing.

Too many Christian men and leaders, try to live on the basis of their past spiritual experience. They are bound for failure. Faith is lived in the here-and-now. Past victories hold fond memories but little muscle for present conflicts. So these men fall into compulsive behaviors and destroy their ministries. God's name and his good work is distorted by the poor reflection these men give.

No amount of spiritual teaching or number of experiences can erase the reality of a man's emotional and spiritual woundedness. Unless a man deals with his father-son wound, he is unable to connect with the emotional and spiritual reality in his heart. And without an emotional connection, he will not feel loved by God. The Christian life cannot be truly lived and experienced when God's love is not felt deep in our hearts.

A man who is detached from his feelings cannot feel the needs of his own Christian community. He has no feelings for the boy in the single-parent family who has no contact with his father. He has no compassion for the elderly widow in his church. He cannot sympathize with her inability to afford or accomplish needed repairs for her roof and windows. He has no feeling for the laid-off father who is about to lose the family home. He feels no need to call or encourage the man. He has no concern for the teenager groping to find his moral compass. He cannot see his need for the security and stability of an older man. He cares little about the boy in Sunday school who is hungry for any contact from an older man who loves God.

Emotionally Connected—Spiritually Activated

A man becomes spiritually alive when he begins to deal with his own woundedness. His emotional connection opens the way for spiritual growth. When Scripture gets to a man's heart, he becomes spiritually motivated. He begins to feel what Christian living is all about. It changes his life. This kind of transformation was evident in the life of Steve, a client who first came to me because he could not stay sober.

For several generations, the men in Steve's family had been work addicts and alcoholics. The women in the family went to church, but the men never seemed to have time for it. Steve was an out-of-control drinker, just as his father and grandfather had been. But a family crisis forced him to make changes. He made a commitment to attend 90 Alcoholics Anonymous meetings in 90 days. He knew it would take intense effort to make a change.

The twelve steps of Alcoholics Anonymous gave Steve an awareness of something bigger than himself. That enabled him to stay sober one day at a time. He started to identify and feel his inner woundedness. This discovery enabled him to make an emotional connection with his wife and kids. For the first time in his life he also made a spiritual connection with God.

Meanwhile, one of Steve's son became an altar boy. I suggested to Steve that it would mean a lot to his son if he would go to church and see him serve. Steve hung his head and said, "I'm too ashamed to go to church."

"Why?" I asked.

"I wouldn't know what to do if I had to look up something in the Bible," he answered. I had never heard anyone say that before.

I sat down next to Steve and showed him how to find verses in the Bible. Then I shared the "big secret" with him. "The truth is," I said, "hardly anybody knows where all of the books of the Bible are! Sooner or later, most of us have to look up one in the Table of Contents!"

He laughed and could hardly believe me. But I assured him that it was truth. I also led him through the Four Spiritual Laws booklet. I encouraged him to read it again and make his own decision. Shortly afterward, Steve decided to ask Christ into his life. His sobriety increased, and he started going to church regularly. Now he goes to church a half hour early so he can meditate before the worship service begins. He reads the hymns and Scripture selections for the service and thinks about them. "You know, Earl," he said recently. "I don't know why more people aren't in church before it starts. It's so quiet. It's the best time all week to focus on my relationship with God. I have to do it. It helps me stay sober and maintain conscious contact with God."

It has been fascinating to work with Steve. He spends time every day praying for his father. And he continues to heal the wounds he suffered in his relationship with him. As Steve works through his father-son wound, he becomes more open and involved with his wife and sons. He has explained to his sons that he is an alcoholic. He talked openly about the things he has done to them. He asked for their forgiveness. He also told them that he is always available to talk with them about whatever they need to discuss. After this, his teenage sons began to open up to him. His amends with his wife and sons created a new closeness and trust that was not possible before.

Steve dealt with the wound in his relationship with his father and opened the way for a deep spiritual vitality. Steve was no longer an emotionally and spiritually detached man. He began to experience and live out the Christian life. Many men go to church for a lifetime and never discover what Steve found.

Like Father, Like God

A man's relationship with his father has a tremendous bearing on his personal relationship with God. When a bond exists between father and son, the son will find it easier to trust his father's spirituality. The son will want to model his father's spiritual life. If a man's relationship with his earthly father has been difficult and distant, he will find it hard to know and trust God. In fact, a little boy's first image of God the Father reflects the image of his earthly father. A strong emotional connection between father and son makes it easier for the son to feel spiritually connected with God. But if no emotional bridge exists, the son may feel that God is distant and disinterested.

Consider these common examples of how a man's relationship with God mirrored in his relationship with his father:

▶If a man's father has been unpredictable or moody, made promises he did not keep, or failed to support him when he needed it, a man does not know what he can count on in his relationship with his heavenly Father.

▶If a man's father has been critical, judgmental, difficult to please, or cruel, a man will tend to view God as a harsh taskmaster who is just waiting for an excuse to punish him.

▶If a man's father has been shaming or demanded perfection, a man will feel hopelessly inadequate before God, compelled to do as much as he can for God, yet feel guilty for never doing enough.

▶If a man's father has been passive when action was appropriate, a man will have a hard time trusting God to play an active role in his life.

▶If a man's father had a strong, macho personality, showed no compassion, and denied or minimized pain, a man will find it hard to believe that God is compassionate and concerned about his pain, struggles, or fears.

All of the emotions that are wrapped up in a man's relationship with his father are also wrapped up in his relationship with God. When those issues begin to heal, a man will experience God in new and different ways. He will feel God's presence in his life. He will trust God's love and pure motives. And he will sense God's acceptance and approval.

This healing process was apparent in Steve's life. His recovery from alcoholism caused him to face the reality of his father's emotional, physical, and spiritual abuse. His father's abuse left Steve with much shame. It was hard for him to even walk into a church. He was terrified of what might happen if he did something wrong. This overwhelming fear of God and church was rooted in Steve's fear of his father, who exploded in rage any time Steve was less than perfect.

Once I understood Steve's relationship with his father, it was easy to understand his difficulty with church. Opening his heart to Christ was a big step. I do not believe he could have taken this step and grown in Christ had he not connected with his father-son wound.

Hope for the Christian Community

I believe that tremendous change can and must take place among men in the Christian community. I look forward to the day when Christian men will feel their spirituality deep in their hearts. I look forward to the day when men will heal enough in their relationships with their earthly fathers to feel a personal connection with their heavenly Father. I look forward to the day when Christian men will rise up in masculine strength and make a positive difference in the Church and the world.

I believe Christian men can fulfill this vision. Years ago, I witnessed what a united masculine community can do. It wasn't a Christian deed in name, but it was in spirit. I was a teenager then. My home was a farm in southern Minnesota.

Toward the end of one summer, a farmer on a neighboring farm became very sick. The other men talked about his health at the gathering places—grain elevator, cafe, and service station. Everyone knew the man would not be able to harvest his corn and plow his fields for the next spring. Before long, a date was set. The entire farming community would descended on the man's farm and get the job done.

Early on that day, two or three combines arrived. Four or five tractors with plows showed up. Then men with trucks and wagons to haul the corn drove in. The giant combines began their slow, relentless advance across the corn fields. Row after row was picked and shelled and stored in the hoppers—mounds of golden corn. Then, one by one, the trucks and wagons pulled near the combines to receive streams of golden corn. Neither combine nor truck ever stopped. They continued to help the man in need. They were driven by urgency—cold weather and snow were not far away. And whatever crop was left would be destroyed. When the combines and trucks had finished and moved, tractors came into the fields. Stalk choppers, disks, and plows worked the land and readied the ground for the next spring.

I remember my feelings that day. I belonged in the world of men—and that made me proud. I still see the men wave and smile and call to each other as they passed in the fields. I still hear the roar of the diesel engines and see the billow of black exhaust when the pulling got tough. I still feel the ground tremble under the weight of all those men and their machines. Many men brought together for one harvest—for one man's crop. At noon they stopped to share a meal. I listened to them talk and laugh and tell stories. Some remembered similar events in the past. Their fathers had done this before.

That event took place almost 35 years ago. Still, the sense of my participation in something very great and good lingers with me today. I will never forget the strength, the unity, the compassion, and the community among those men that day. I also felt a special confidence and comfort deep in my heart—I knew that same kind of help would be there for me if I ever needed it. I didn't know it then, but what I witnessed that day was an example of masculine spirituality. I saw what it means for one man to help another. I experienced something of God's love that I had not known.

I remember that day with a certain sadness too. That strong, masculine spirituality was not easy to see in everyday life. I knew there was an underlying sense of caring among the men of that community. Still, there was no outward and direct expression of that care unless a crisis forced it out. Most of those men were Christian, but their faith was silent and private—just like their emotions.

These men desired a strong spirituality—I know that deep inside. But they lacked a way to express it openly. This is one of the sad legacies of the father-son wound. For generations, spiritually passive men never find the fire in their belly that could move them to become active participants in the Christian community. They never find what it takes to touch the hearts of the wounded, widowed, and poor as Christ did. But this legacy can change when men take courageous and painful steps to grieve their wounds and seek healing in the company of other men.

A Closer Look

Emotionally and Spiritually Detached—A man's emotional detachment from the world around him contributes to an empty and fruitless spiritual life. A man numbed to his emotions is also numbed to spiritual feelings. He can know in his head that God loves him. Still, he must experience what it *feels* like to be loved by another person. Without the emotional experience of love, it is impossible to feel God's love.

Spirituality—An excellent definition of spirituality comes from the twelve-step programs. In these programs spirituality is defined as being in proper relationship to the truth. That truth begins in God, as we know God in Christ and in the Bible. But there is also a truth about ourselves with which we must come into proper relationship. It is the truth that denial and other "figs leaves" have hidden from us. We say in recovery that "you are as sick as your secrets." It is true. Spiritual people are freed by the truth that they uncover and embrace.

Masculine Spiritually—When men allow their hearts to be moved and their wills to be united in concern for others, they can express a masculine spirituality. God's love can move men to takes action so long as their hearts are open and responsive on an emotional level. They will respond uniquely as men in male strength and unity, and they will accomplish tasks that would have been impossible for the women alone.

Distorted Image of God—As I noted in the chapter, a man absorbs his father's spirituality. He learns about God the Father through his relationship with his earthly father. Thus the emotional, physical, and spiritual wounds he suffers in his relationship with his father have a direct impact on his connection with God. Those wounds leave distortions about his heavenly Father. His spiritual health and the state of his soul will depend upon his willingness to process and move beyond these distortions.

How do we heal our image of God? A book, *Divine or Distorted? God As We Understand God*, was written for this need. In it, author and pastoral counselor Jerry Seiden says:

> *"You thought I was altogether like you!"* These are God's words, found in Psalm 50:21, when he spoke to the injustice and delusion of the day. Think of it: a God who is just like us. No thanks! That's backward. We don't want a God who is like us. We want to be like God. An important distinction emerged between the God of Israel and the gods of the ancient world. Few ancient peoples wanted to be like their gods. Godliness was no virtue. Remember how capricious, immature, and cruel the Greek gods of Olympus were? Or what of the Roman's gods? Worse yet, would anyone want to be like Molech, the god of the Ammonites, who demanded that children be sacrificed by fire? To be godly would be cruel, unfeeling, and immoral.
>
> However, the opposite was true in Israel. God was good. And he wanted his people to be like him. He said again and again, *"Be holy for I, the Lord your God, am holy!"* So in Psalm 50, God points out a grave mistake: the assumption that God is like us.[2]

Personal Reflection

1. Describe the current condition of your spiritual life.

2. In what ways do you relate to the idea of emotional and spiritual detachment?

3. In what ways is your current spiritual or religious life different from or similar to your father's?

4. In what ways did your father's behavior or attitudes toward you affect your understanding of God?

5. What examples of masculine spirituality can you recall from your past experience? How did these experiences affect your life?

NOTES:

CHAPTER 7

Masculine Growth and Recovery

Masculine growth is a recovery process for most men. It demands courage and commitment. It takes integrity for a man to admit his inner need for healing. It is not easy to face the pain of the father-son wound. A man must be willing to deal with the deep, unresolved issues in his life. It takes grit and guts for a man to recognize that he is vulnerable and he is not invincible. The only untouchable men of steel are in the comic books or on the movie screens.

No man wants to invite this kind of grief. It hurts all the way through. The tears that come are beyond control—normal defenses no longer work. For a time, a man in recovery cannot manage his emotions. His tears may flow for any number of things with no apparent rhyme or reason. He feels things he has never felt before.

To open, expose, and explore emotions is not an easy experience for a man. No matter what his age, a man must redefine what it means to be masculine. Everything he thought he knew about being a man is up for grabs. This uncertainty creates insecurity—even a little insanity. But the discomfort will pass.

Every step a man takes toward masculine growth is a step in the right direction. Once the door is open, there is no turning back. It may be a wild ride, but the reward is worth it. He will discover what it means to be a man. He will find and form deep relationships. He will experience spirituality that touches his very soul. And he will undergo deep and lasting change.

Growth and the Little Boy Inside

Inside every man there is a child. The little boy inside is still in touch with all the emotions (painful or pleasant) surrounding his relationship with his father. Few adult men have ever had an emotional connection with this little boy. Some men have disassociated themselves from the childlike part of their nature. They appear to be very "adult." They are controlled, not playful. They are unable to laugh freely or have fun.

Other men are moved by the whims of their childlike part. They appear to be immature and self-centered. They pursue their own pleasures to the exclusion of their families. They fail to take on their responsibilities as fathers and husbands. Both types of men have not connected with the little boys within them. As a result, they live as victims of their father-son wound—completely unaware of it. As we have seen in previous chapters, that wound affects their work, their friendships, their family life, their community life, and their relationship with God.

For a man to heal his father-son wound, he must reconnect with the little boy inside. When he does that, he builds an emotional bridge between his adult self and his inner feelings. He is then able to deal with the sadness, grief, anger, and other deep emotions related to his father-son wound.

Consider how Dave changed when he connected with the child inside. Dave began counseling because of deep depression and recurrent panic attacks. He was a kind and likable man. But he was somewhat passive and had difficulty expressing his feelings.

One of the first things I asked him about was his family. Dave was the youngest of three boys. He was born rather late in his parents' life. His next oldest brother was ten years older than he was. As Dave grew up, he rarely heard from his brothers. His father held a variety of jobs—everything from cowboy to merchant marine. His mother was protective of her youngest son. Still, the whole family was rather disconnected and detached. No one had much of anything to say to anyone else. No one shared their feelings openly.

After I learned about Dave's family background, I asked him to picture himself as a little boy. He closed his eyes and immediately burst into tears. Just the visualization of himself as a little boy brought him to grief. He was overcome by the emptiness and loneliness he had experienced when he was young. I then asked him to imagine his adult self stepping toward the little boy and holding him close. This process brought out even more emotion.

The sobs and sorrow confounded Dave. His emotional reaction was a new experience. It did not match up with his view of masculinity. Dave believed that big boys don't cry. Jesus was supposed to wash away all the pain. Men are supposed to handle their problems on their own. Dave's image of tough, self-sufficient masculinity shattered. The reality of his inner pain burst through his conscious experience. He came face to face with the overwhelming sadness and grief of a little boy inside. The boy knew his father loved him, but he had never felt the warmth of that love. He had never felt the depth of his father's care.

Dave walked through this valley of grief, and he began to make sense out of his panic attacks and depression. He got in touch with the sorrow that the boy inside felt over what he had missed in his relationship with his dad. He was able to mourn the loss of his father, who died while Dave was in his early 20s. He felt the sadness, confusion, and fear of all the years he lived without a dad to talk to. His father was already gone when he married and became a father. Dave realized that despite a successful career and approaching retirement, he felt very young, fragile, and afraid.

Dave's connection with the little boy inside connected him to the deep wound he suffered in his relationship with his father. This is where the father-son wound begins to heal. But it is important to realize that this is just the beginning of healing, not the whole process. The process of healing continues as a man deepens his relationships with other men and with God.

Growth Is Not Achieved Alone

A man cannot heal the father-son wound alone. A lifetime of messages have told him that real men "go it alone." But those messages are wrong. The business of connecting with inner feelings and healing is accomplished in the company of other men.

It is not easy for a man to find the support he needs. Other men may not be in touch with their own feelings. A man's pastor may not understand the needs of a man in recovery. And unless a man is very fortunate, his father will not understand it either. Even his best friend will not understand unless he is going through the same thing. So a man may feel very lonely and scared until he connects with men who understand and support him.

The men who can help another man in recovery are those willing to be vulnerable and open. They must believe that a virtue vital to manhood is honesty. They must be willing to hear the honest sharing of others without judgment or advice. They must be willing to tell the truth about their fears, failures, weaknesses, and daily struggles. They must see this kind of openness not as a weakness or spiritual defect, but as a positive characteristic of growth. They know that becoming a man is a lifelong challenge—a way that is not mapped out for any man. They know that every man is covering new ground all along the way. And it is not always easy to know which way to go.

The concept of men sharing with men is nothing new. Primitive societies, such as certain tribes in Africa, the aboriginal cultures of Australia and American Indian tribes, have long legacies of initiation and training. In these cultures, men do not function solely on their own. The individual man is a part of the whole male community. The men hunt and fight together. The men nurture and initiate the younger men into their circle. The camaraderie, support, and strength of a united community of men (and women) is essential to the survival of the culture.

In scripture we see the strength and support male relationships can provide. Some men seem guided by God to carry out solitary lives. But those men—like Abraham, Elijah, and Joseph—were the exceptions, not the rule. Most men who were used by God had close relationships with other men. It seems that some men—like Lot, Samson and Jonah—would have gained much from close, supportive relationships with godly men. It is clear that others, like King David, were better people because of their close connection with other men.

During the early and turbulent years of King David's manhood, he enjoyed the covenant friendship of Jonathan. These men were powerful warriors, yet they were very close spiritually and emotionally. They shared their deepest concerns with each other. And neither one was afraid to risk his life for the other.

There is no evidence that David's son, Solomon, ever had such a friend. All of Solomon's great wisdom and his dramatic spiritual experiences did not fill the loneliness he felt inside. In the emptiness of his life, Solomon wrote:

> Two are better than one,
> because they have a good return for their work:
> If one falls down,
> his friend can help him up.
> But pity the man who falls
> and has no one to help him up!
> Also, if two lie down together,
> they will keep warm.
> But how can one keep warm alone?
> Though one may be overpowered,
> two can defend themselves.
> A cord of three strands is not quickly broken (Ecclesiastes 4:9-12).

I wonder how Solomon's life might have been different if he had even one close friend. He needed someone to encourage him, comfort him, and stand by him during his struggles. The support of a close friend might have kept him from the mistake of a thousand wives and concubines. Perhaps he would not have been led to worship their idols. A close friend may have strengthened his devotion to the one true God.

It is helpful to think about the positive male relationships revealed in Scripture. It is important to consider the truths their examples uncover. I see great benefits in the close, supportive male relationships of the Bible. It is interesting that even Jesus did not work by himself. He was able to do miracles, and spoke to the multitudes. Still, he chose to minister in the close company of 12 select men. They learned from his public and private teaching. Later Jesus sent them out in ministry, but not alone. He sent them in teams of two. In his hour of personal need, Jesus asked three of those men to be with him in the Garden of Gethsemane. On the night he would be betrayed, he asked his three closest friends to support him in prayer.

Female Relationships Don't Nurture Masculine Growth

It is easy for some men to seek out women to meet their spiritual and emotional needs for relationship. But a boy can only become a man through relationships with other men. Only men can welcome a boy into the world of men. Only men can share their struggles, failures, responsibilities, and dreams with him. They show a younger man how to live as a man in each new stage of life. Only men can guide, encourage, and nurture a man along the path of masculine growth.

This truth is difficult for mothers and their boys to accept. A mother may become aware of the need in her son's life. She may perceive his pain in his relationship with his father. And she may try to fill that void with extra portions of mothering. In response, the son finds it easy to gravitate toward his mother. Her warmth and sensitivity feels good to him. But the well-intended mother cannot fill the gap. The boy's emotional movement toward his mother will lead to a toxic, codependent relationship between mother and son. This only adds to the son's problems and pain.

Obviously the single-parent mother is in a tough spot. Try as she might, there is no way she can fill all of her son's emotional needs. The situation grows worse if the boy's father does not spend time with his son, fulfill his emotional responsibility, and become involved in his life.

A boy who is over-mothered and under-fathered has real problems. That is why the relationship between a mother and her teenage son can become explosive. A mother may do everything that she knows is right, and still lose her son in some way. He may ignore her when he reaches his teens. He may be disrespectful to her. Or he may even become violent and abusive toward her.

What is happening in situations like this? The son is trying to break away from his emotional dependence on his mother. At some point he needs to do that. But he cannot make a successful break unless he has contact with older men. He needs men who will take an active interest in him. He needs men who will support him along the way as he grows into manhood. Men within the Church can fill this need. If a strong community of men exists, godly men can make themselves available and pick up where a father has failed.

All boys raised in single-parent or two-parent homes need to make an emotional break with their mothers. This emotional break does not mean that young men no longer love or care about their mothers. It means that they need to separate themselves from their mothers emotionally. They need to deal with their own issues. They need to see the world through their own eyes rather than through their mothers' eyes. It means mothers must make a conscious, and perhaps painful, effort to let go of their sons. Mothers must allow their sons to become men. This emotional break sets sons free to become part of the community of men.

It is not easy for a son to make this emotional break with his mother. He cannot do it alone. It takes solid relationships with a number of men for the break to be successful. A son needs more than just a relationship with his father. He needs relationships with uncles, grandfathers, and other men who are close to the family. He needs their help to leave the world of childhood and enter the world of manhood. Consider the roles that each of these important men can play in a man's ongoing maturity.

A Boy Needs His Grandfather

Every boy has a place in his soul that only a grandfather can fill. The grandfather is usually the first older man (other than the father) to whom a boy becomes connected. An older man speaks from a storehouse of experience—a lifetime of learning. He made it through the rigors of life. Through his years he has cried, laughed, loved, and lived to the fullest.

A grandfather who had a rich and passionate life seems to command respect from his family. He imparts a stability and wisdom that only he can give. A true patriarch and grandfather has achieved a balance in the emotional, spiritual, and physical aspects of life. He has much to give to the younger members of his family. Grandfather does not walk on water. But the solid, masculine influence of a godly grandfather is important to a boy maturing into manhood. All men need the infusion of the masculine strength that an older man can provide.

Many boys have lost the opportunity for a relationship with their grandfathers. Many older men do not understand that God designed children with a need to share intimate experiences with their grandparents. A grandfather may not realize that his grandson hungers for such a relationship. Or he may think that holiday visits and family functions are enough. Those gatherings of the generations are certainly significant but more is needed.

Grandfathers must build an emotional bridge to their grandsons. That emotional bridge does not exist on its own. Grandfathers must take steps to build it by being involved in their grandsons' lives. Perhaps the greatest gift a grandfather can give to his grandson is time. He can give him time to share a walk, bait a hook, share a concern, teach a skill, or just to listen. Where distances or finances make regular interaction difficult, the relationship between grandfather and grandson can be nurtured through phone calls and letters.

It means so much when a grandfather maintains an emotional and spiritual relationship with his grandson. It is a rich resource for the grandson throughout childhood, teenage years, and adulthood. A grandfather can influence a growing boy in ways that a father cannot. A young man will take advice and counsel from his grandfather. Yet that same word might not even be considered if it came from his father.

Today one in two marriages end in divorce. A stable relationship with a grandfather comforts and strengthens a boy or young man. When life is full of turmoil, a grandfather can bring balance and offer a solid footing.

Uncles Can Make a Difference

Uncles provide their own brand of nurturing. They have an advantage. They are one step away from the immediate family, yet very close to it. They are both close yet distant enough to trust.

My mother's brother often took time out for me when I was growing up. Sometimes he came to my basketball games. When he entered the service, he wrote letters to me—just to touch base. I wrote back to him. It never seemed to matter to him what I was up to or how crazy I was. He always accepted me. He was always willing to listen. His faithful acceptance and loving concern made it possible for me to accept constructive criticism from him. I would have rejected it from other older men. Even today, although we live in different parts of the country, we still talk about anything. It means a lot to me to be able to share my thoughts and struggles with him. I share my worries about making a living and being a father. And I get to hear how he has struggled with some of the same things.

I was also privileged to have known my great-uncle, Bill Henslin. I wrote about him in a previous chapter. He had already turned his farm over to his sons by the time I was a teenager. He always seemed to have time to talk. He was a tall, gentle man. He entered politics when he was in his late 60s and served several terms as mayor of Dodge Center, Minnesota. I remember how he talked with everyone we met on the streets around town. He offered a warm handshake, a caring smile, and often a mischievous wink. It all communicated his sincere interest in what was important to the people he encountered. In some ways, he was like a father to the whole community.

Bill's life was filled with rich relationships. Everyone had an almost immediate admiration and respect for him. His interest in his adult children, grandchildren, great-grandchildren, nephews, nieces, cousins, grandnephews, and grandnieces never waned. He was active and involved in his family and community until the day he died. Just to be around Bill and talk with him was contagious. Boys, young men, and grown men soaked up his values, attitudes, and feelings. His gave us all pieces of himself—things that are crucial to living life.

Sadly, most young men today do not know what it is like to have a significant relationship with an uncle. Many men I have counseled do not even know the names of their uncles. And few uncles realize the positive impact they can have on their nephews' lives. Uncles have no idea how much a card or phone call can mean. They do not know how to build the kind of relationship with their nephews that will help them grow into manhood.

Men Outside the Family

All men who are close to a boy's family could help to nurture his masculine development. It is a tremendous blessing when an older man outside the family takes an interest in a boy. But it is rare these days. There is little unity or understanding among men regarding their masculine role as a group. The community of men within the Church and in society at large is underdeveloped. It is also rare for individual men to make the personal commitment necessary to nurture young boys. As a result, boys seldom have the support of other men. They attempt the necessary emotional break with their mothers all alone.

Albert lived across the road from my parents' home. As long as I can remember, he took an active interest in me during my childhood. About age five or six, I began to cross the road to talk with Albert. He always had time for me—no matter what. Sometimes he would stop his work, sit down, and talk. Other times he would let me follow him around while he did chores.

As I grew older, I continued my trek across the road to see Albert. My teenage years were filled with the normal confusion and bewilderment of that age. But in Albert and Ann's house, I always felt accepted. College years were busy. Still, I continued to visit Albert whenever I came home. It felt good to know he was there willing to talk. He showed interest by asking all the right questions. I relished the chance to tell him about my major or the activities I enjoyed.

I took my firstborn over to meet Albert. Ben was just a baby, but I thought it was important to introduce the two. Ben accompanied me on some of my visits when he was older. I wanted my son to know an older man like Albert. His warm and caring nature made him special. In time, Ben began to visit with Albert on his own.

Albert was generous to those who were younger than himself. He lived a simple life in his small, white clapboard house. He worked hard in his garden despite chronic arthritis in his knees and hips. He drove an old Chevy, but had four snowmobiles for play. He and his grandchildren enjoyed fun in the snow together.

Several summers ago, when Albert and Ann were well into their 80s, Albert gave me a precious gift. He may not have even realized the gift he gave me. He enabled me to see what a marriage commitment meant at the other end of life. I crossed the road to visit early one morning. I found him in the garden—hard at work. We talked for some time, and then he asked, "Would you like to see

Ann before you go? She won't remember your name," he explained. "She may confuse you with your brother. And even if she recalls your name, she might ask who you are a few minutes later. Don't let it worry you none. It's just the way things are now."

Albert's solid commitment to love and care for his wife had endured through many years. They had good times and tough times. They enjoyed health and endured sickness together. And now, in the late winter of their years, he carried the load—alone. He suffered physically, but Albert cared for Ann at home until his strength was gone. It was very hard for him to put her into a nursing home. She died there just a few months later. His faithful, caring commitment was a strong testimony to me. I was impressed by how much he loved Ann and by what marriage meant.

Albert died on the day of his wedding anniversary. I learned from others that I was not the only man he entertained. Many men from the community had frequent visits with him. Albert touched a whole community of men, from young boys to men in their 60s. Men wanted to spend time with Albert. He had a way of making a man feel loved and cared for. It did not matter who you were or what your age. He could reach across the gap and greet you. We need men like Albert today. We need older men who know how to nurture and who know how to love.

Every Man Needs A Friend

Most men have not had a close friend since their teens or early 20s. Career developments and family concerns take priority in their mid 20s. There is little time left for cultivating relationships with other men. But the need for other men to surround them and support them is the same throughout life. Relationships with other men enable a man to deal with reality. They help him stay focused on what is important. And they encourage him to invest his life in what truly matters.

I often suggest to the men I counsel that they need the support and closeness of other men. And they often look at me in shock and disbelief. The idea of an intimate, emotional and spiritual relationship with another man is beyond their comprehension. The idea is foreign to them because of their father-son wound. And when men become aware of this wound and feel their loss, they begin to view other men as allies and resources for greater personal growth. They realize that good friends are crucial for masculine growth.

A Closer Look

Masculine Growth—The masculine growth discussed in the chapter above in not an automatic development like puberty. Real masculine growth is a recovery process for most men. This sort of development was not available during their formative years. It requires that a man face the pain of his father-son wound. To open, expose, and explore emotions is not an easy experience for a man. No matter what his age, a man must redefine what it means to be masculine. Everything he thought he knew about being a man is up for grabs. This uncertainty creates insecurity—even a little insanity. But the discomfort will pass. He will discover what it means to be a man. He will find and form deep relationships. He will experience spirituality that touches his very soul. And he will undergo deep and lasting change.

Inner Child—The little boy inside a man is that part of him that is still in touch with the pain and losses of his childhood. It is that part of him that still waits for a relationship with his father. It is that vulnerable and needy part of him that wants to be comforted and held. It is that part of him that needs protection and healing.

Personal Reflection

1. How would you describe the needs of the little boy within yourself?

2. Did your mother try to compensate for parenting not provided by your father? In what ways did you break free from your mother's influence?

3. Describe the relationships you had with your grandfathers.

4. Describe the relationships you had with any uncles or older male members of your extended family.

5. What close male relationships do you have today? If you have none, make a list of men who you believe would be of support to you. Is there anything that would prevent you from calling any or all of these men to arrange one-on-one times of fellowship?

NOTES:

CHAPTER 8

Bridges of Healing
Between Father
and Son

S everal years ago, my father asked if he could attend a seminar that I was leading on the father-son wound. I was a bit surprised by his interest. Still, I was happy that he wanted to come along. As the seminar began, I explained that I wanted to honor three special men in the group. I introduced them one by one.

The first was Will Hawkins, M.D. He was also my seminar co-leader. Will has been a close, supportive friend through nearly 20 years. Those years were a mixture of good and painful times. But Will has remained a compassionate and caring friend. I have seen God use him to heal people in body and bless them in spirit.

The second was Bob Bartosh. He and his wife Pauline are the founders of Overcomers Outreach. An Alcoholics Anonymous member with 26 years of sobriety, Bob has modeled Christ's love and acceptance. He has stuck with me through all kinds of situations.

The third man I introduced was my father.

All three men are in their 70s and each has been a father to me. God has used them to touch deeply my emotions and spirit. One man is my birth father. One man is an emotional father and a solid mentor in my business and profession. His prayers and encouragement have sustained me in difficult times. And one man has been a fatherly role model. His life is a demonstration of the honesty and strength found in a twelve-step recovery program.

As I introduced these men, I was overcome with emotion. Grief overpowered me and sent tears rolling down my cheeks. I was captured by my sense of loss in my relationship with my father. I saw him with the two other men—the contrast was heart-wrenching. The relationship that I had with Will and Bob is what I desired to have with my father.

My father's eyes were also full of tears. They came from his own deep sadness and emptiness in his relationship with his father. And I know he had tears for me and for the sadness I carried. At that moment, it did not matter that I cried in the presence of a hundred men. What mattered was that God had given me a precious gift. I had the chance to see my father shed tears for me.

Fathers Are Wounded Too

My father's acknowledgment and expression of pain in that meeting was necessary for my healing and for his. Healing will not occur between father and son unless the father is willing to face his own woundedness. But this is a foreign concept for most men. The son must also recognize and accept his father's woundedness. This can occur only after the son has experienced some healing of his own.

It is important to remember that the little boy within all men desires affirmation, approval, and acceptance. We can say to ourselves, *I've done a great job.* But we long to hear that praise from men who are important to us. Nothing beats hearing our fathers say, "Son, I'm proud of you."

Like most men, I knew my father cared about me. Still, I never heard him express those feelings to me. Consequently, I felt frustrated and hurt in my relationship with him. I also felt ashamed for having those feelings. After all, I knew in my head that my father loved me. Why couldn't I feel it in my gut? That gut-level experience was necessary for me—as it is for every man and boy.

It dawned on me that my father did not know how to express his love for me. He had never experienced such love from his father. I began to recognize that the little boy within him was as wounded as the one within me. My grandfather had been unable to express that he loved my father and valued him as his son.

In fact, many of my grandfather's actions showed favor to my father's brother and rejection of my father. My grandfather's actions communicated that my father was inadequate and not to be trusted with responsibility. He was made to feel unworthy of blessing or reward. The final crushing blow came when my grandfather died and left the entire estate to my father's older brother. My father's brother confirmed the message of my father's unworthiness by accepting the entire estate. He shared none of it with his brother. Their combined actions conveyed a terrible, shaming message to my father. He was rejected despite years of working side by side with his father and brother. My father was wounded deeply—as any man would be.

I am proud of many things in my family, but this story is not pretty. For healing to occur, the dark side of that woundedness must be recognized and accepted for what it is. My father has begun to recognize his pain. He can see how the lack of expressed love by his father wounded him as he grew. As a result, he is trying to be more open and expressive toward family members. He tells us how he feels and does not assume that we already know by his actions.

The key to healing the father-son wound is for men to begin to experience their own feelings. They must bring out the deep wound within them and learn to share the pain of that wound with other men. When men do this, the stage is set for them to develop relationships on a much deeper level. As part of my own recovery, I had to go through stages of grief and anger. I had to deal with what I had not received, and probably would never receive, in my relationship with my father. I faced my own woundedness and began to see my father's. I was able to accept him for who he is. This acceptance is a necessary step in building strong emotional bridges between fathers and sons.

Like Father, Like Son

Doug had worked hard to provide well for his family. He grew up with an alcoholic father, who only worked during brief periods of sobriety. Doug hated the shame of growing up on the wrong side of the tracks. His shame was magnified because his family lived in a small town where everyone knew everything about everyone. As a teenager, Doug vowed that his children would never suffer the way he had.

Doug kept his vow. His family did not suffer because of a lack of material things. They suffered in other ways. Doug traveled extensively for his job, and when he was home, work was his first priority. He always had a pile of paperwork to complete. And that kept him from spending time with his son, John. Although he never said much about it, John missed his father's time and attention. In fact, when he was a teenager, John bitterly vowed that he would never work the long hours his father worked.

Like his father, John kept his vow. He was home by 4:30 every afternoon. He never missed a school conference. He attended every ball game, was present for every camping trip, and took part in every special program. But something was not quite right in John's life. He came to me for counseling because of deep depression.

John was fully involved in his children's activities, but he seemed unable to connect with them on a deeper emotional and spiritual level. John did not realize it at first, but he responded to his children with the same emotional coolness he had experienced in his relationship with his father. He never had an emotional connection with his father. And he could not give his children what he did not have.

John progressed in counseling. He connected with the grief he bore from the lack of closeness to his father. He shed many tears over the losses in that relationship. His grief work enabled him to relate to his children on an emotional, spiritual, and physical level.

In time, John realized that his relationship with his father was the primary issue he needed to resolve. He asked his father to join him in counseling. Through our counseling sessions, Doug began to share his feelings about John's lifestyle. He did not feel that John was working hard enough for his family. He feared that John would not have enough money to send his children to college. He wished that John lived in a better neighborhood. He even hated the old car John drove!

Can you see what was happening? John had chosen a different lifestyle than his father had chosen. He provided for his family but did not accumulate wealth. In a pattern typical of the grandchild of an alcoholic, John had chosen to grow in the experience and expression of his feelings. His greatest desire was to be a family man involved in the lives of his wife and children. The choices John had made triggered many of his father's unresolved issues.

In subsequent sessions, Doug began to feel the pain of what he had missed in his relationship with his father. He discovered within himself a shamed little boy who had been embarrassed by his father's alcoholism and neglect for his family. He also grieved over what he had lost in his relationship with his son. He realized he had been somewhat jealous of the time John spent with his family. He felt shamed because he had not spent more time with John when he was younger. Without realizing it, Doug had refused to face those feelings in himself. Instead, he directed the anger and sadness he felt in his relationship with his father toward his son.

It was a special moment when Doug felt the sadness of his son's loss and John felt a deep compassion for his father. Both men shed tears for the other. By feeling each other's pain, father and son experienced an emotional bond they had never known before. John became free to honor his father for providing for his family. Doug gained a new respect for his son. He was set free to recognize John's need to live out the values that were important to him. This freedom and growth in intimacy would never have taken place if Doug and John had not risked experiencing the grief of their father-son wounds.

An Adult Son Needs an Emotional Bridge to His Father

If men are to be fully men, an emotional bridge between father and son must exist. Doug and John made tremendous strides in their masculine growth. They worked through their respective father-son wounds and established an emotional bond. Their new intimacy enabled them to gain a respect, admiration, and acceptance for one another that they had never experienced before.

Every man would benefit from an emotionally intimate relationship with his father. Every man has a deep longing to be honored, respected and admired by an older man. If a man has a father who can give of himself emotionally, God has given him a great gift. Unfortunately, few men today have received this gift. So it is important that men seek out older men who can play an active role in their lives.

Robert Moore is a psychologist who has done extensive writing and speaking on men's issues and the full scope of masculine development. He has said that a man is wounded if he is not admired by an older man at least once a week.[1] I wholeheartedly agree. By participation in my life, Will Hawkins, Bob Bartosh, and Bill Henslin have admired me. That high regard has helped heal my woundedness. I look up to these men and see something in their lives that helps me grow. When they compliment me or respond to me, they touch the wounded little boy within. When I listen to their words, my soul is enriched. In turn, my listening honors them. My respect reminds them that their struggles in life have been worthwhile.

The father of an adult son can be sure that his son has a deep desire to hear his expression of love. He wants to know, without a doubt, that his father approves of him as a man. A man who does not affirm his son on a continual basis further wounds his son. It is never too late to begin this process. Never too late to say, "I love you." Or "I'm proud of you." No matter how old a son is, healing can begin with simple affirmation and approval from his father.

A Father Needs Support for Building a Bridge to His Son

A father, aware of the wound with his own father, can feel sadness for the loss his son has suffered. The father's own grief prompts him to seek an emotional connection with his son. Many fathers are relieved to know it is never too late for a father to build that bridge.

But building an emotional bridge to an adult son is no easy task. The process carries significant emotional risk for both father and son. To handle those emotional risks, it is important that a father be well established in his own recovery. He needs a strong support group for himself before he reaches out to his adult son.

Support is necessary because many fathers feel a great amount of guilt and shame when they realize how they have wounded their sons. At times this guilt is so great that a father will stop making progress in his own healing. But if he has the support of other men, they can help him focus on his continued growth. They can help him learn to forgive himself and move on.

The idea of forgiving oneself is very important. On his own, a man cannot father a son on a deeper emotional level than he experienced from his father. A man must give himself grace as he seeks to build an emotional bond with his adult son. He has to realize that he is just like every other man in the world. He must learn how to be a father. The support of other men is invaluable as he grows into new levels of fatherhood.

A father also must give up the notion of perfection. It simply cannot be done. The only perfect Father is God. A father needs to accept the reality: his best efforts will not fully meet his son's needs. Some fathers, for example, must spend significant time away from home and children to do their jobs. Even when a father is home, he cannot meet every emotional need. I have four children. I can only be emotionally available to one child at a time. That means I'm unavailable to the other three at any given moment. It is easier to accept my limitations as a father when I have the perspective and support of other men.

Also remember that it has only recently become acceptable for men to recognize and express their feelings. Emotional awareness is a new experience for many men. It is particularly difficult for those who grew up in the 30s and 40s. Until recently, the reality of masculine emotion was considered unimportant. Even principles put forth in most Christian parenting books ignored the child's and the parent's feelings. Since such a fundamental aspect of father-son relationships has been ignored, it is no wonder that a great emotional gap exists between most fathers and their sons.

The active support of other men can help a father understand, sort out, and express the feeling side of his masculinity. They can help him take steps toward healing in his relationship with his adult son. They can also help him handle the ups and downs of his son's responses as he moves closer to him.

A son may respond with anger, resentfulness, or silence to his father's emotional overtures. In this case, support for the father is essential. A man can be hurt when he does not receive the desired response from his son. A hurt father may relapse into anger, shame, and rejection of his son. But a father with the support of other men can express his frustration and hurt to them. His support group can encourage him and pray with him. They can ask God to open a door in his son's heart. They can help the father bear the pain of building an emotional bridge to his son.

Building a Bridge from Father to Son

After honest evaluation of their existing relationship, a father must approach his adult son with great care. Some fathers have a good relationship with their adult sons. So a move toward emotional intimacy deepens and enriches what they already enjoy. Other fathers have never been close to their adult sons. So their overtures may be greeted with suspicion or resentment. They will have a more difficult time establishing an emotional bond with their sons. Some fathers have been physically or emotionally abusive so their sons may respond with distrust and rage to any contact. These men face a long and difficult road.

A father must never forget that he cannot control the process of healing in his relationship with his son. Healing of the father-son relationship will not occur unless the son is open to the process. The longer the emotional bridge between father and son has been down, the greater the son's anger, suspicion and resentment toward his father. Denial or addiction may cause a son to reject his father's attempts at establishing an emotional relationship. That is why a father must set good boundaries. A father who seeks to build an emotional bond with his son cannot take his son's initial reaction personally. Nor can he afford to be defensive. Both of these common responses are destructive to the healing process.

A father must not offer excuses for what has happened in the past. Excuses mean nothing to an adult son who has been hurt. A father needs to take responsibility for the ways in which he has wounded his son. He must express his deep sorrow for having done harm. And he must hang in there while his son works through what ever emotions the father's approach has unleashed.

Some fathers have been uninvolved in their son's life for a long time. In this case, the son may respond with frustration, defensiveness, or denial. The reason for this is clear. Inside the adult son is a little boy. He's waiting to see if the involvement his father now promises will really come to pass. While the son was growing up, there might have been periods when his father was close to him. But then a promotion came along, and the father started working long hours again.

A father cannot expect years of woundedness to be brushed aside because he wants to make amends. A father must give his son time to work through his anger and sadness related to their relationship. A son needs time to learn how to trust again. It may take a month, six months, or even longer for the son to work through his mixture of feelings. Waiting through this process is never easy. Still, a father must remember that dealing with the anger is part of the process. The anger will not last forever. The son simply needs a season to grow and heal.

Waiting for a son to work through his emotions is particularly hard for Christian fathers. Christians tend to think that if we apologize, others should immediately forgive us and everything should be okay. The truth is, nothing in Christianity equates human forgiveness with trust. Forgiveness and trust are separate issues. Forgiveness is a one-time action a person chooses to make. Trust is a cumulative result of experiences over time.

Therefore, it is important that a father remain emotionally available to a son who is working through loss and grief. If a son greets his father's movement toward him with distrust and anger, it is easy for a father to back off and close the door to further intimacy. Yet if a father is far enough along in his own recovery, and has the support of other men, he can remain emotionally close to his son during this difficult time. A father can listen as his son expresses the deep emotions he feels regarding their relationship. He can acknowledge and accept responsibility for the ways in which he has hurt his son. Also he can establish firm boundaries within himself so that he does not accept blame for wrongs he has not committed.

One reason boundaries are important is because a son may become abusive as his father moves toward him emotionally. A father must not allow himself to become a victim of his son's anger. He may need to say to his son, "I am here to talk with you about your anger and hurt. I want to listen to you, but I won't allow you to yell at me or abuse me."

In this type of situation, support is crucial. A father may need to find a third person, such as a pastor or therapist. He may need someone knowledgeable about these issues and willing to be involved in the reconciliation process. More and more frequently, I receive calls from parents who express distance from their adult children. They want to rebuild those relationships and need help to do it. There is nothing wrong or shameful about seeking the help of others. The healing process between father and son covers a lot of new ground, and emotional reconnection is sensitive.

A father may need the help of a third person if there was sexual abuse in the son's life. The wound of sexual abuse goes deeper into a man's soul than all other wounds. It destroys a man's trust in other men. A son who has suffered sexual abuse may be extremely resistant to establishing emotional intimacy with his father. This is true even when someone other than the father was the abuser.

A son who has been sexually abused may not be consistent in his relationship with his father. The father may think their relationship is going well. Then, suddenly, his son may withdraw or become angry. A father must not take his son's inconsistent response personally. This response may stem from the wound of sexual abuse and not the wound of the father-son relationship. All fathers need to be aware of this possibility and have a strong support system available so they can deal with it.

I cannot emphasize enough how important it is for a father to have the steadfast support of other men. A father must have other men with whom he can share his feelings as he moves toward greater emotional intimacy with his adult son. Their support will strengthen the father's boundaries. A father who takes steps on his own, without any support, may be devastated by his son's response. He may withdraw or revert back to old ways of relating to his son.

Practical Steps for Building Bridges

A father takes a tremendous step when he bridges the emotional gap between himself and his adult son. The impact of his previous actions may cause him to wonder, *Where do I start?* There is no "right place" to begin. A father can take steps toward emotional intimacy with his son in a number of different ways. It all depends on the kind of relationship he already has with his son. Their physical distance plays a part too.

One father and son began by attending a men's conference together. This made it easier for them to begin talking. The structure allowed them to discuss deep issues that had been too awkward to approach. Recently, the father called his son and said, "You know, since the sale of the business, I have time to do more things. I know you're busy, but I'd really like to go skiing with you. We haven't done that since you were a teenager! If you can get away for a few days, I'll pay the airfare." That man's son was thrilled. He responded like an enthusiastic little kid. He rearranged his work schedule so he could go. The two had a great time together.

Most adult sons are not used to their fathers initiating joint activities. It makes a tremendous impact when the father says, "Let's go camping. Let's do something together—just you and me. We'll have a chance to get to know each other better." Fathers should be aware, some sons may show no interest in the activities their fathers initiate. In that situation, the father must accept his son's choice, but he should not give up. He should wait for a while and then extend another invitation. The son may be waiting to see if his father will really follow through in the relationship.

For some fathers and sons, a weekend together would be too much time to spend with each other—at least at first. If that is the case, a father can invite his son out for lunch. I know one adult son who never misses a lunch with his dad. The father listens to his son and then prays with him about what he is going through. The son benefits from his father's time and attention. He also benefits from the blessing of his father's prayers.

If physical distance between a father and his son is a problem, phone calls, letters, or e-mail can open a deeper relationship between them. A father need not overdo it to the extent that he bothers his son. Still, he can express interest in his son's life. A father's calls and correspondence may pave the way for spending more time with his son.

All of these steps can help establish an emotional relationship through which a father and son can address their deeper issues. When the time is right, the father can initiate a discussion with his son about the past—the times when he wounded him. He can express sorrow about the hurt and harm done. He can take responsibility for making amends. From that point on, the son's response determines the father's next step toward emotional intimacy. If the son's response is openness to further sharing, the emotional bridge is beginning to be established.

Building a Bridge from Son to Father

Every young son needs his father to reach out and establish an emotional bond with him. This is not something a child can do for himself. His father must do it for him. Many fathers have not done this, nor do they have a clue that an emotional bridge between father and son can or needs to exist. Some adult sons, however, have become aware of their need for an emotional bond with their fathers. They want to make it happen. These adult sons have already come face to face with their father-son wound. Their own recovery efforts depend upon a deeper emotional level. They have felt the loss of a relationship with their fathers, and they desire to develop an emotional bond with them.

I assure adult sons that it is possible, but not ideal, for them to initiate the risky first steps toward their fathers. I urge sons to use great caution. We have already seen how risky this reaching out can be for the father of an adult son. It is an even riskier step for the son to take.

It is essential that the adult son be in a strong recovery program before he attempts to reach out to his father. This means that the son must deal with the grief of his father-son wound. He must develop solid, emotional relationships with other men. He must learn how to deal with the painful memories of his relationship with his father. He must develop boundaries in his relationships so that he does not fall into old, harmful patterns.

A strong, ongoing recovery program and adequate support are particularly important if a man's father is in denial or unaware of the significance or depth of the father-son wound. A father who is in denial will probably not give his adult son the emotional response he seeks. This can devastate a man who is reaching out. A son without adequate support may relapse into his addictions if the father responds with shame or control. If some openness already exists in their relationship, the father's response is less likely to harm the son.

An adult son who wants to establish an emotional bond with his father is wise to respect the positive benefits his father has tried to provide through the years. He should also recognize and appreciate his father's predicament. Most fathers faithfully provided for their sons' material needs and had no idea that their sons required anything more. Some fathers sacrificed greatly, denying their own needs, in order to provide for their families. My own father has lived through years of pain from arthritic knees and a bad back. Both are the results of the hard physical labor he performed on the farm. I need to feel the value of the sacrifice he made for me. But recognition of the father's past sacrifices does not take away a son's pain. Still, it is important that at some point the son be able to value the good his father has given to him.

An adult son must never forget that his father also bears a deep wound in his relationship with his own father. He must recognize that his father's wound has influenced how he relates to his son. A son may go through a time of grief for his father when he recognizes that a wounded little boy also resides within his father. If the father has suffered sexual abuse, the son may need to accept the fact that his father may never be the father he would like him to be.

Very few fathers have had the opportunity to discover the feeling side of their masculinity or to recognize their own woundedness. Men as a whole are just beginning to discover what a feeling masculinity is all about. Most fathers need to be educated about these issues. They may have no idea what recovery is all about. In the minds of many fathers, recovery is something that happens to the economy, not to people. To them, recovery is what you do after you have bypass surgery.

I take this need for education into account when I counsel a father and son together. I explain that this is an opportunity for both of them to learn something new. I assure the father that he cannot be expected to know how to do something he has never experienced himself. A father is usually responsive when approached this way. I can then talk about the grief in the hearts of men. I describe the grief that comes when a father shames his son and when he withholds his blessing. When I begin sharing stories of the grief in men's hearts, it is rare for a father not to connect with his own inner pain. Often the door is open for father and son to share together and cry together. They connect with each other's grief, and their relationship is forever changed.

Change Doesn't Mean Perfection

It is a special moment when a father and son share some of their grief together. It is rich when they begin to build an emotional bridge between them. This does not mean, however, that all is well in their relationship. If a father and son desire to continue building their relationship, they have a great deal of work to do. Both must deal with the old hurts and new challenges of their life together. This is not an easy thing to do. They must proceed with patience and commitment.

A father and son who want to strengthen their emotional bond must not expect perfection. Both of them will make mistakes that hurt the other. This kind of hurt is difficult to deal with when the relationship has been strained and stretched. When a misunderstanding arises, or when the father or son relapse into old patterns, it is easy to assume that nothing in their relationship has changed or ever will. In these situations, the father and son need to remember that God alone is perfect and unfailing. They need to remind themselves that some things in their relationship have changed and that other changes will occur if they continue to work at it. A father and son must be patient as they rebuild their trust in each other.

Rebuilding trust requires an agreement to deal with the old hurts that undermine their relationship. A man does not fully trust a man who has hurt him in the past. So healing of these old wounds must take place before the new father-son relationship can grow. Healing takes place when a father or son share openly about hurts and resentments. Healing occurs when one man knows that the other man wants to hear him and respond to his pain. One adult son told his father how humiliated he had felt as a teenager when his father had teased him. His father did not become defensive but acknowledged how he had hurt his son without intending to do so. He then told his son he was sorry and promised that he would try to never shame him again. This type of sharing strengthens the emotional bridge.

Healing between father and son will not occur if old, hurtful feelings are ignored or pushed away. A father and son must learn how to express their feelings directly. Most men make mistakes as they learn this new skill. So they must be patient with one another. As a father and son bring the pain of past wounds out into the open in a safe way, they can respond to this pain with genuine sorrow and forgiveness. And the emotional bridge between them can grow much stronger.

However, no father-son relationships are perfect. A father and son may hurt each other as their relationship deepens. It is important that fathers and sons trust one another enough to directly express their feelings about current wounds as well as old ones. When I turned 40 years old, every member of my family congratulated me except my father. I was already saddened by the fact I was leaving a decade of my life behind, and my father's apparent lack of interest added to my burden. After two weeks had passed without a word from him, I wrote my father. I told him that I had been hurt because he had not called me or sent a card. When my father received my letter, he called right away. His voice was sorrowful and his tone apologetic. He said he was sorry that he had hurt me. We talked about my sadness and about his sadness as well. As we connected with our feelings, my anger and resentment toward him lifted. It was not easy for us to talk about these feelings. Still, we have agreed to do so because it is the only way we can continue to grow in our relationship.

Strengthening the bond between fathers and sons is not all work. Fathers and sons who want to continue to build their relationship need to take time for what my son and I call "men's stuff." Men's stuff is whatever a father and son do when they take the time to enjoy an experience together. For some fathers and sons, this may be an all-day fishing trip. For others it may be a backpacking or whitewater rafting trip. Or it may be sharing a meal together and going to their favorite baseball team's opening game. For my son Ben and me, men's stuff is the Rosarito-Ensenada bike ride.

Ben and I have taken this 50 mile bike ride together every year for the past several years. We even went, via tandem bicycle, the year Ben broke his arm a few days before the ride. The route winds along Mexico's Pacific coast, then climbs from sea level to 1,200 feet in a grueling 8 mile stretch of switchbacks. When I'm pedaling up that stretch, I always wonder why I do it. But I wouldn't trade anything for the exhilaration of standing at the top with my arm around Ben, basking in our conquest. After the ride, we head for the beaches and cliffs where we play and relax until nightfall. Then we shoot off the fireworks we picked up along the way. This kind of men's stuff is great for strengthening the bond between father and son.

Bridge-Building for a Lifetime

The father who becomes aware of his own woundedness while his children are still young has an advantage. It is even better if he understands this before they are born. This father has the opportunity to think about what he wants in his relationship with his son. He can make the choices that help ensure a close relationship from infancy through adulthood. He can take the daily steps in the healing of his own father-son wound that will enable him to build a bond with his son.

A father who has plunged into the reality of his own pain will feel more deeply what it means to be a father. He will be much more sensitive to his son's feelings. A father who is emotionally connected with other men for mentoring and support will find it easier to be emotionally close to his son. He will grow into fatherhood and be able to share his worries, fears, and dreams about being a father. A father who is emotionally close to another man, whom he admires as a father, has a valuable resource for dealing with the practical, day-to-day problems of fathering. The son of such a man will be fortunate indeed.

As the son grows, he will have a father who knows how good a loving hug at the right time feels—even to a teenager. He will be able to talk to his father about almost anything. He will have a father who sincerely cares about things that are important to him. He will have a father who makes promises his son can trust. A father who deals with his woundedness has the hope of passing on these and many more gifts to his son.

No matter what stage or age, it is helpful for a man to realize the importance of building an emotional bridge between generations. His efforts may represent the first time in generations that any healing interaction has taken place in the family. Such a step is truly historic. It may be the first time two generations of his family have connected on a deep emotional level.

When a man takes such a step and sticks with it, his decision will have a positive impact upon his family for generations to come. Building emotional bridges requires tremendous courage and occurs only after a man has passed through the painful process of facing his own woundedness. But the man's children, grandchildren and even great-grandchildren will feel the rewards of such an effort. Such a man leaves a legacy that will be felt for many years to come.

A Closer Look

Resentment—Resentment is a major roadblock to recovery that must be removed. Resentment is the bitterness and anger we feel toward those whom we perceive as threats to our security or well-being or those who have caused us harm. If not removed, our resentments act as anchors and hinder our progress and growth.

Denial—Denial is a key survival skill. We protect ourselves by not admitting that anything is wrong. We ignore the real problems by replacing them with a host of elaborate explanations, rationalizations, and distractions such as minimizing, blaming, excusing, generalizing, dodging, attacking, etc.

Modeling—Values are imparted from one life to another. *Values are caught not taught.* Models are the living examples of character that impact another human being—for good or evil. The whole direction of a person's life is set by his values. We pay attention to what we value. Christian discipleship is an example of positive modeling and value impartation. Another positive example is the sponsorship one finds in twelve-step programs. But the most important modeling takes place in the home from parents to children. Like it or not, children look to their parents' behavior for the most important lessons of life. Words are not needed. Modeling imparts values through conduct, attitudes, behaviors, and beliefs.

Support—The support that heals and helps us is the support we get from others—individuals who share our problems, pains, and struggles. We cannot make it alone. It is tempting to remain silent when we deal with deep, painful issues. But that silence can be deadly. The support and safety of others is needed to break the silence and speak the truth about our lives. The support of others can direct our focus away from painful circumstances and onto recovery and positive action. We need a support-ive group of others who recognize our struggles, who can grieve with us, who will see us through the lonely times, and who will affirm our values.

Personal Reflection

1. Who are the most important men in your life today?

2. Do you feel safe with and respected by your father?

3. In what ways has your father modeled appropriate boundaries? What has he done to encourage you to develop your own personal boundaries?

4. In what ways are you and your father able to share deep and difficult feelings with each other?

5. What are the "difficult issues" you have faced with your father?

NOTES:

CHAPTER 9

Nurturing Masculine Growth for a Lifetime

W hen a man begins to deal with the pain and issues related to his damaged relationship with his father, he has a increased capacity to develop his masculine potential. Masculine growth is much more than a man healing his relationship with his father. Masculine growth entails the development of a man's whole being—spirit, emotions, talents, and accomplishments. It entails the development of a man's potential at every stage of life—husband, father, spiritual leader, master in his vocation, and wise and generous elder.

Masculine growth is an intimidating process. The good news is that it is not supposed to happen overnight. It is not the result of one event, and it is never complete. It is intended to be a lifelong process. *Most important, it is a process that must be nurtured through relationships with other men.* The process of men encouraging and nurturing masculine development in other men is called *initiation.*

Initiation Isn't What You Think It Is

To most American men, the word initiation conjures up images of Boy Scout ceremonies, secret rituals, or bizarre fraternity hazings. None of these things nurture the kind of lifelong support that causes masculine growth. The true concept of initiation is unknown in our culture today. The type of initiation that fosters masculine development can still be found in the practices of various tribal societies.

In aboriginal societies that practice male initiation, there comes a time in a boy's life when the older men take him from his mother and bring him into the world of men. The men of the tribe make a symbolic and physical break between the boy and his mother. He usually does not see her for an extended period of time. Then following his initiation, he will never live with her again. The boy's initiation is often an intense training time. His physical, emotional, and spiritual skills are expanded and tempered. He may have to accomplish difficult tasks. He may be required to go through a time of fasting. He may have to endure pain—in the presence of the men of his tribe. These activities take place within the context of ritualistic ceremonies in which the whole company of men participates. These ceremonies involve the telling of legends that communicate the history of the tribe. There may be songs, dances, chants, or poetry that glorify the heros of earlier generations. Depending on the tribe, the initiation process may take several years to complete.

It is easy to see how this process would cause a boy to feel that he belongs in the world of men. This type of experience instills the values, history, and traditions of male society into a boy's soul. It teaches a boy that the men of his community are a valuable resource to him.

Ray Raphael assesses the function of primitive tribal rituals. Here is how he describes what initiation accomplishes:

> The most important and sweeping function of a primitive initiation was to provide a youth with a sense of his own personal significance within the context of a greater world. In becoming a man he took his place alongside his father and forefathers; by discovering his tribal heritage he became connected with the ongoing flow of life. He was transformed into a spiritual being as he joined his ancestors in a universal brotherhood that cut through time.[1]

Robert Bly interprets the significance of initiation for men today:

> "The ancient societies believed that a boy becomes a man only through ritual and effort—that he must be initiated into the

world of men. It does not happen by itself, it does not happen just because he eats Wheaties. And only men can do this work.[2]

We have abandoned the process of initiation in American culture today. That is a tragic loss. Fathers and older men no longer nurture boys into manhood. Instead, boys are left to their own devices. The result is devastating. In the introduction of *To Be a Man,* Keith Thompson notes the harmful results of this loss:

> When a culture ceases to provide specific, meaningful initiatory pathways, the individual male psyche is left to initiate itself. And therein lies a great danger, visible in the kinds of initiation to which many men turn: street gangs, drug and alcohol abuse, high-risk sports, militarism, discipleship to charismatic cult leaders, obsessive workplace competition, compulsive relocation of home and job, serial sexual conquests, pursuit of the "perfect" (and thus unattainable) older male mentor, and so forth.[3]

In the same book, Robert Moore and Douglas Gillette comment on the personal pain some men suffer because of this missing element in male development:

> A man who "cannot get it together" is a man who has probably not had the opportunity to undergo ritual initiation into the deep structures of manhood. He remains a boy-not because he wants to, but because no one has shown him the way to transform his boy energies into man energies. No one has led him into direct and healing experiences of the inner world of the masculine potentials.[4]

For most men, masculine potential remains a mystery. The impact of a solid community of physically, emotionally, and spiritually developed men on our society remains unknown. Initiation has been absent from our culture for so long that men do not know what it is. And all of us—men, women, children—suffer from its absence.

The Need for Initiation Today

Families, the Christian community, and society do little to recognize the stages of a man's development. They do even less to nurture his growth through those stages. What little initiation we do have is at best superficial. Consider the following common milestones of a young man's growth in society today:

▶**Driver's License**—It is a big step when a young man gets a driver's license. Still, a driver's license provides little more than legal access to an expensive, lethal weapon.

▶**Catechism and Confirmation Classes**—Catechism and confirmation classes have some of the characteristics and potential of initiation. Yet for most young men, tire potential of these experiences is lost. Why is this so? First, a young man often endures these classes only because his parents make him do it. Second, those who teach the classes are often unaware of the potential for deep growth and take a superficial approach to the process. Third, the community of men in the church may not model or actively support the principles and values that are taught through these classes.

▶**Varsity Sports**—The high school varsity team is an accomplishment many boys anticipate. They look up to the juniors and seniors on the team and admire them as men. The boys feel that participation with the varsity elite would make them more than boys. Team sports give a sense of belonging and camaraderie, but they do little to nurture emotional and spiritual growth.

▶**Sex**—Many men (young and older) consider themselves to have arrived at a manhood when they have sexual relations for the first time. Unfortunately, this often occurs prior to marriage.

▶**High School Graduation**—Graduation from high school is a true milestone. It is an opportunity to nurture a young man's maturity at a deep level. This passage is recognized through a formal ceremony, but deeper nurturing rarely takes place. Graduation often becomes an excuse to attend an all-night party.

▶**College**—A young man goes off to college and begins a new era of life. With the exception of professors or coaches, most young men are cut off from the nurture and influence of older men. In the absence of the older generation, young men turn to peers who also need nurturing. It is easy for a young man's life to take bizarre twists.

▶**Military Training**—The initiation experienced in military training is a young man's best opportunity for real growth. Basic training is designed to be a growth-producing process. The instructor's job is to push his recruits hard to expose what they are made of. The tough training tests their physical and emotional endurance. At the end of training, men usually celebrate together. They have earned the right to join other men in military service. They have an undeniable bond with a whole group of men.

It is easy to see how these forms of initiation fall short of what young men need. They offer little impact on a deep emotional level. God created young men with a need to be trained and nurtured into their full masculine development. So the need for initiation is still very much a part of every young man's being. When initiation is absent, young men seek it out on their own.

Jay, for example, found his own initiation into manhood through his use of cocaine. As a teenager, he felt empowered when he used the drug. His feeling of importance was enhanced because he used cocaine with older teenagers. Acceptance in their group gave him a sense of placement in the world of men. Other uninitiated young men may turn to gangs, crime, or the pursuit of sexual experiences as a way to achieve acceptance and status as men. True initiation is not an option. It is a necessity. But none of the false initiations described above accomplishes what young men need.

As young men grow into manhood, they need the active involvement of older men who have wrestled, suffered, and grown into their own masculine identity. Our society desperately needs what these older men have to offer. But there is a dire shortage of spiritually and emotionally alive men who recognize the need and have the willingness to nurture masculine growth in younger men.

Initiation an Function for the Christian Community

I believe the community of Christian men need to become involved in the process of nurturing men. Christian men have not considered it their business or responsibility to nurture one another or to nurture young men. Still, they acknowledge their spiritual need for discipleship. Initiation and discipleship are not as different as we might think. It is appropriate and necessary for Christian men to actively nurture masculine development.

The Christian community of men can help a young boy become

a man and guide him along his lifelong physical, spiritual, and emotional journey. Christian men who are committed to God can help a young man go through the painful process of making an emotional break with his family. They can help him discover an identity apart from his family. The strong support of a community of Christian men can help a young man mature into the spiritual and relational responsibilities of manhood. Christian men can affirm, encourage, and challenge one another to discover and cultivate their spiritual gifts. When the time is right, a young man can take his place among his peers in the Christian community and help initiate those younger than himself. And he can still continues to be nurtured by the older men of the community.

Scripture is full of illustrations about initiations that nurture a man's development. Let us consider the major elements of initiation that are evident in the lives of several well-known Bible characters.

Movement from Parents to the World of Men

The first major steps a young man takes as he develops into manhood is an emotional break from his childhood. He must emotionally separate himself from his mother and step into the world of men. For many young men this is a difficult step. The prophet Samuel was a fortunate young man. He was born under unusual circumstances to parents who had a strong spiritual commitment. As a result of their commitment, his parents helped him enter the world of men. Look at his story.

Hannah, wife of Elkanah, had been barren for many years. One year, when Hannah and Elkanah were at Shiloh to offer their annual sacrifice to the Lord, Hannah prayed earnestly for a child:

> In bitterness of soul Hannah wept much and prayed to the LORD. And she made a vow, saying, "O LORD Almighty, if you will only look upon your servant's misery and remember me, and not forget your servant but give her a son, then I will give him to the LORD for all the days of his life, and no razor will ever be used on his head" (1 Samuel 1:10-11).

Eli, the priest, saw her praying and rebuked her—he thought she was drunk. She explained that her fervent prayers came from her great sorrow—she had no child. He sent her on her way with the words, "Go in peace, and may the God of Israel grant you what you have asked of him" (1 Samuel 1:17). In due time, Hannah gave birth to Samuel.

The first year after his birth, Hannah did not take Samuel to Shiloh for the yearly sacrifice to God. Elkanah was ready to fulfill his vow, but he knew Hannah had to fulfill her commitment to God in her time. She asked him to let her wait until Samuel was weaned. Notice his beautiful response to her request: "'Do what seems best to you,' Elkanah her husband told her. 'Stay here until you have weaned him; only may the Lord make good his word" (1 Samuel 1:23).

Hannah kept her commitment. While Samuel was still a very young child, he was brought to the temple to train for his lifelong responsibilities. This turning point in Samuel's life was not made casually. It was marked by a significant ceremony.

> After he was weaned, she took the boy with her, young as he was, along with a three-year-old bull, an ephah of flour and a skin of wine, and brought him to the house of the LORD at Shiloh. When they had slaughtered the bull, they brought the boy to Eli, and she said to him, "As surely as you live, my lord, I am the woman who stood here beside you praying to the LORD. I prayed for this child, and the LORD has granted me what I asked of him. So now I give him to the LORD. For his whole life he will be given over to the LORD." And he worshiped the LORD there (1 Samuel 1:24-28).

It was no easy task for the family to travel to Shiloh. It probably took several days. It also wasn't easy to kill and sacrifice a three-year-old bull. It certainly was not easy for Hannah and Elkanah to let go of such a young child. Yet the ceremony was appropriate in light of the significance of the break being made between Samuel and his family. Hannah and Elkanah were acutely aware that they were giving their son back to God. From that point on, Samuel would continue the process of training and development for God's service, with Eli as his mentor.

In Luke 2:41-52 we see an emotional break from the family take place in Jesus' life. Every year Jesus and his parents went to Jerusalem for the Feast of the Passover. But when Jesus was twelve, he stayed in Jerusalem to listen to the teachers in the temple. His parents assumed that Jesus was traveling with other family members. For a full day they did not know that he was missing. Once they knew, they went back to Jerusalem and searched the city for three days. They found him in the temple. Notice his parents' response to the situation:

> When his parents saw him, they were astonished. His mother said to him, "Son, why have you treated us like this? Your father and I have been anxiously searching for you."
>
> "Why were you searching for me?" he asked. "Didn't you know I had to be in my Father's house?" But they did not understand what he was saying to them.
>
> Then he went down to Nazareth with them and was obedient to them. But his mother treasured all these things in her heart. And Jesus grew in wisdom and stature, and in favor with God and men (Luke 2:48-52).

Jesus created some turmoil in his family when he went off and did what he had to do! He had reached a point in his life where he needed to be with the teachers of the Scriptures. He was no longer a boy. Led by God the Father, he was taking a step away from the world of his parents toward the world of men. This step did not please his parents. They did not understand it and were worried about him. Still this step was necessary for Jesus to grow "in wisdom and stature, and in favor with God and men."

At some point, the normal spiritual and psychological development of a boy requires a movement beyond the world of his parents. To develop as a man, a young man needs to become more independent of his parents. He needs to step into his place in the world of men. The Christian community of men can play an important role in directing and nurturing this difficult stage of a young man's life.

Initiation: A Movement through the Stage of Life

To develop to full potential, men need preparation and direction through the various stages of life. When a man marries, his life is different from what it was when he was single. When a man owns a company, he faces demands far removed from that first job as a teenager. When he becomes a father, he relates to his children in a different way than he related to childhood playmates. A man is fortunate to receive the nurture and encouragement of other men as he develops through these stages of life.

A series of events in David's life show his progress in becoming a man. Like Samuel, he also had an initiation into manhood. He was clearly set apart from his family. It is interesting that Samuel was the man who initiated David into his adult role. This event occurred when Samuel anointed David to be the next king of Israel (see 1 Samuel 16:1-13).

God directed Samuel to anoint one of the sons of Jesse to take Saul's place as king of Israel. But God did not tell him ahead of time which son he was to anoint. As the youngest son, David was his family's least likely choice. In fact, he was not even invited to participate in the selection process. I can imagine the pain he must have felt to not be remembered by his father. One by one, David's seven brothers stood before Samuel, but the Lord had not chosen any of them. Finally, Samuel had to ask if there were any more sons in the family. When David was brought to him, "the Lord said, 'Rise and anoint him; he is the one.' So Samuel took the horn of oil and anointed him in the presence of his brothers, and from that day on the Spirit of the Lord came upon David in power" (1 Samuel 16:12-13).

There was no denying the significance of what had happened in David's life when Samuel anointed him. But this was just the beginning. Samuel did not say to David, "You've been anointed, so let's tell Saul to take early retirement so you can take over." Instead, David continued to grow and mature. He faced a number of initiatory experiences and stages of life that prepared him to become king.

One of the most famous of these experiences occurred when David went to the battlefield to deliver food to his brothers. There he encountered the giant, Goliath. David had fought against wild animals to protect his father's sheep. But this battle, with a man, would be his initiation as a warrior of Israel. When given Saul's armor and weapons, David found that they did not suit him. Instead he defeated Goliath with his sling and a stone. After his victory over Goliath, David spent many years fighting the enemies of Israel. This was an important stage of life that helped prepare him for his future role as king and protector of Israel.

David also spent time living in the king's household. He served Saul and was a part of his daily life. During those years of close contact with the king, David learned what it meant to be a ruler. In his early experience with Saul, David watched a healthy, powerful king conduct the nation's affairs and protect the nation from oppressive enemies. Later, David also had the opportunity to see how *not* to be king. He saw a great king of Israel lose sight of God's calling and direction for his life. David watched as Saul's character deteriorated before his eyes.

Other examples of initiation in Scripture demonstrate how a mentor can guide a younger man into a new stage of development. On his second missionary journey, Paul took Timothy under his wing. For a time, Timothy helped Paul in his ministry. Then Paul left Timothy in Ephesus with instructions to continue the work they had started. Timothy was young for the challenge and responsibility of leading the church at Ephesus. Paul knew this and continued to mentor him from a distance. Paul wrote Timothy the two letters that bear his name in the New Testament. The Apostle's words helped Timothy fulfill the duties of his new leadership role.

Eli also had direct responsibility for initiating younger men into God's service. Eli had failed to initiate his sons into their God-ordained role. That failure had dire consequences for the priesthood and Eli's family (1 Samuel 2:27-36). Still, Eli was faithful to initiate Samuel into his God-ordained role as a prophet of Israel.

Initiation Develops the Whole Man

An important purpose of initiation is to nurture the growth of the whole man. When a man's masculine growth is nurtured, all dimensions of his being will develop more fully. For instance, we know that as a warrior David had great physical strength and endurance. We also know that he had highly developed creative abilities. He was a skilled singer, harp player, and song writer. His music provided comfort for king Saul when he was troubled by evil spirits.

David's spiritual side is better known than his ability as a warrior and musician. His reputation as a "man after God's own heart" has stood throughout the ages. His psalms express an honest, vulnerable, deep, unfailing relationship with his heavenly Father. In his relationship with God, David holds nothing back. He expresses a full range of emotion and spiritual feeling—depression, praise, hate, sadness, shame, and joy. At times David struggled with honesty and integrity. Still, he maintained a direct and feeling relationship with his heavenly Father.

Older men help nurture a man's professional, emotional, and his spiritual growth. Part of this nurturing involves helping a man hear the voice of God. An event in the lives of Samuel and Eli illustrates this process. Samuel was about twelve years old:

> Then the LORD called Samuel. Samuel answered, "Here I am." And he ran to Eli and said, "Here I am; you called me."
>
> But Eli said, "I did not call; go back and lie down." So he went and lay down.
>
> Again the LORD called, "Samuel!"
>
> And Samuel got up and went to Eli and said, "Here I am; you called me."
>
> "My son," Eli said, "I did not call; go back and lie down."
>
> Now Samuel did not yet know the LORD: The word of the LORD had not yet been revealed to him. The LORD called Samuel a third time, and Samuel got up and went to Eli and said, "Here I am; you called me."
>
> Then Eli realized that the LORD was calling the boy. So Eli told Samuel, "Go and lie down, and if he calls you, say, 'Speak, LORD, for your servant is listening.'" So Samuel went and lay down in his place.
>
> The LORD came and stood there, calling as at the other times, "Samuel! Samuel!" Then Samuel said, "Speak, for your servant is listening" (1 Samuel 3:4-10).

On his own, Samuel could not discern the voice of God! He could not tell the difference between Eli's voice and God's voice. Only through the wisdom of Eli's experience did Samuel learn how to hear God's voice. I think this story has a powerful message for Christian men today. It shows the need for men who have experienced a lifetime of listening to God. These men can help younger men draw near to God and discern his voice.

Eli also helps Samuel learn another vital lesson that will equip him to carry out his future role as God's prophet. Eli impresses upon Samuel the necessity of being honest and truthful, even when it is painful to do so. He told him to disclose the whole message that God had given him. It was a devastating for Eli, Samuel's his beloved mentor:

> "At that time I will carry out against Eli everything I spoke against his family—from beginning to end. For I told him that I would judge his family forever because of the sin he knew about; his sons made themselves contemptible, and he failed to restrain them. Therefore, I swore to the house of Eli, 'The guilt of Eli's house will never be atoned for by sacrifice or offering'" (1 Samuel 3:12-14).

Samuel did not want to give Eli bad news. But he could never have carried out his future role as prophet if he had not learned to listen to the voice of God and to proclaim His word at any costs.

These are not the kinds of lessons a man learns on his own. None of these stages and aspects of masculine development occurred without the input of other men. Samuel had Eli who, over a period of years, helped usher him into his role as prophet. David had Samuel to whom he could run in his time of need. He also had the opportunity to observe Saul when he was still a great king. Timothy had Paul who ministered with him side by side and who continued to instruct and guide him in his new responsibilities.

A man needs relationships with a variety of men throughout his life to continue his masculine growth. A man needs men who will initiate him through the stages of life. A man needs others who will nurture the development of all aspects of his masculinity. This is no less true today than it was in biblical times.

A Closer Look

Initiation—The process of initiation encourages and nurtures masculine development in men. It provides a young man a sense of his own personal significance within the context of a greater world. In becoming a man he takes his place alongside his father and forefathers. He becomes connected with the ongoing flow of life. The ancient societies believed that a boy becomes a man only through ritual and effort—that he must be initiated into the world of men. It does not happen by itself. And only men can initiate other men.

Personal Reflection

1. What worldly experiences have you had with initiation? Did you participate in any activities or rituals that were supposed to "make you a man"? What do you feel that you gained?

2. What positive experiences have you had with initiation? In what ways do you feel that your masculine growth was nurtured?

3. At what point in your life did you experience a separation from the world of your parents? What were the circumstances, benefits, and challenges that faced you?

4. What supportive friends, older men, or mentors nurtured your transition from parents to the world?

5. At this point in your life, what do you feel you still lack in your masculine development? What could other men give you?

NOTES:

CHAPTER 10

The Nurturing Role of Male Mentors

No father can possibly be everything to his son. Nor can a father fill every one of the needs a son has as he grows into the ever-changing roles required by his relationships to his family, church, profession, and society. Since a maturing son has a real and legitimate need for guidance and support in all of these areas, the son needs relationships with men other than his father who will help initiate him into adult life. A boy who is becoming a young man is fortunate indeed if he has relationships with older men who will help him in this way.

One of those vital relationships with older men is with a mentor. A mentor plays a critical developmental role in a young man's life. The right mentor can nurture every aspect of masculine growth. He can help a young man develop his full potential spiritually, emotionally, and professionally. A mentor steps in to fill some of the needs a young man's father cannot fill. He plays a key role in helping the son heal from the woundedness of his relationship with his father.

What Exactly Is a Mentor?

Samuel Osherson, a Harvard psychologist, has conducted extensive research on male mentoring. Notice how he summarizes the mentor's role:

> A mentor is a more senior, usually older, person in the world

of work who serves a transitional function for the young person, helping him to become established in the adult world of work yet also nurturing his own special values and beliefs. More people *think* they have mentors than actually do in the true sense of the term: a close *nurturing* relationship between old and young in the work world. Given the nature of the workplace, the mentor is usually a male, particularly for men.

The mentor serves very important, healthy functions in helping the younger person mature into adulthood. Dr. George Vaillant has examined in detail the lives of successful men from college through later adulthood in what has come to be called the Grant Study. He found the presence of mentors central to men's career success and to their maturation as people. "The new role model of the late twenties and early thirties seemed associated with the acquisition of solid career identification." Men with relatively unsuccessful careers either had not discovered mentors until their early forties or had mentors only in adolescence.

The mentee, too, serves an essential function for the mentor: By nurturing the younger person, the mentor keeps alive his own values and hopes, which helps him deal with his mortality and allows him to develop more "generative" parts of himself. Indeed, many men find that the mentoring relationship at work allows them to heal some of the wounds of parenting; feeling frustrated with their own children, some men turn to their younger colleagues as "surrogate sons."

Daniel Levinson, one of the most careful students of the mentoring relationship, writes that "the mentor relationship is one of the most complex, and developmentally important, a man can have in early adulthood."[1]

I would add that the mentor relationship is important not only during early adulthood, but throughout a man's life. No man ever outgrows the need for a mentor. In fact, men need many mentors during the course of life. A vocational mentor is essential for helping a young man find his way in the business world. Another mentor may be primarily spiritual. Another connects with a man and listens to his family concerns, helping him feel and respond to his wife's and children's emotional needs. Still another may step in as a middle-aged man contemplates a risky step, such as quitting his job in order to go back to school or planning a career change.

Does the Mentor Relationship Look Like?

One of my first encounters with a mentor was with my great-uncle, Bill Henslin (the man I mentioned in chapter 8 who, late in life, was elected mayor of his Minnesota town). He was quite a man. Unafraid to make changes in his life, he was his own person. Still, he was solidly rooted in his relationships with family.

Bill gave me an incredible gift: the sense that he had as much time for me as I needed. In fact, he was that way with everyone. He never seemed rushed or hurried. He always wanted to know how I was doing. He asked questions about my activities and plans, and I knew he listened. His warm smile and lively eyes conveyed his sincere interest in me. Bill was always there to follow my progress: high school, college, marriage, graduate degree, fatherhood, move to the West Coast, and doctorate. Without fail, he was wanted to talk, tell a few jokes, and share a few struggles.

Each time I came to town, I would find Bill involved with people. He might be with a group of men at the grain elevator, in the tavern playing cards and drinking coffee, or at the service station. An old man with deep lines in his face that mark the years. He fit there in his position in the community—chief encourager and listener. He had a way of connecting with just about everyone—a neighbor, the teenager in trouble, even the "very important" people in town. Bill was a gentle and warm man who loved to laugh. He had an impact on everyone with whom he was involved. His kindness and hospitality gave me a glimpse of God's goodness. When he placed that big hand of his on my shoulder and smiled, I knew he cared about me.

Bill showed me some of what it meant to be a successful old man. He had grown through the struggles, pain, and fears of life without destroying his relationship with God, his wife, or his children. He was faithful to the principles that governed his life. His rock-solid values never shifted, no matter what popular opinion might be. He was straightforward, sometimes blunt, in sharing his wisdom. At other times, he would simply listen and stand by me. His quiet, mature strength could encourage without a word.

In college I met Dr. King, a solid Christian who became a mentor early in my professional life. He had an outstanding reputation among students. The word on campus was, if you had to take a psychology class, try to get it with Dr. King. My experiences with him taught me that it was possible to be a Christian and to be involved in the field of psychology.

Although he taught at a state university and could say little about his faith in class, Dr. King would often hum or quietly sing hymns as he walked about campus or waited for the classroom to fill with students. When classroom discussion centered on a topic that pointed to the need for spiritual insight, he would ask the students whom he knew were Christians to share their ideas. I admired his ability to communicate the message of Christ within the limitations of his position. His boldness and genuine warmth touched everyone who had contact with him. I often met with him after class to talk about Christianity and how Christian beliefs fit in with psychology. He was a great help to me in the process of maturing as a man, as a Christian, and as a psychologist.

As I continued my schooling, my practicum supervisors also became mentors to me. Dr. Benedict Cooley expressed a warmth and concern that I had experienced only occasionally before in my relationships with men. The freedom and relaxed confidence he exhibited as he shared about his spiritual life with his clients also impressed me.

Dr. Klimek prodded me toward deeper masculine growth. He challenged me to look deeper, both into myself and my clients. He made it clear to me that my clients would be limited in their personal growth if I limited my own growth. He not only challenged me to grow, but through his own life modeled a deep commitment to ongoing personal growth. He also exhibited great confidence in his intuition and helped me become more confident in mine.

More than a professional mentor, Dr. Klimek was also a remarkable father. He was very much at ease with his children and had an unusual ability to accept their uniqueness while at the same time setting firm boundaries for their actions. The outer appearance of the family was less important to him than was his children's freedom to develop their individual personalities. When I spent time with Dr. Klimek and his wife, I noticed a deep warmth and caring between them. They seemed to genuinely enjoy being together. As I got to know him better, I grew to admire his actions as a man, as a husband, as a father, and as a therapist. He was a mentor to me in all of those areas.

When I moved to California to pursue my doctoral degree, Dr. Bill Hunter became another mentor in my life. He and his wife Florence worked at the school I attended and consistently offered emotional support. Their help at that time in my life was very important. My wife Karen and I had two small children, and I seriously wondered if I would be able to make it through the program and provide financially for my family. A man close to my father's age, Dr. Hunter touched the little boy inside me. He listened to my worries and warmly expressed his confidence in me. His consistent encouragement helped me to hang in there and continue growing in my profession and in my faith in God.

During the past several years, my most significant mentoring relationship has come through the experience of sharing an office with Willard Hawkins, M.D. Will has modeled excellence in his practice of medicine. He has helped me learn what is involved in operating a financially successful practice. He has also modeled an unwavering commitment to tithe a portion of his earnings to God. Through Dr. Hawkins' support and guidance, I have grown in all of these areas. Yet he has provided much more than advice and a model of excellence. He has been able to listen to my deep feelings and respond to them in a way that encourages strength, boldness, and confidence.

I feel privileged and grateful to have been mentored by all of these men. Each one offered his unique support, encouragement, accountability, and wisdom. This support enabled me to continue growing in all aspects of my manhood. No earthly father could ever have given to me what these men together gave me. No man on earth can guide, direct, and nurture another man in every area of life.

This was an important truth for me, and all sons, to learn. I have come to realize that I expected my father to be able to do everything. I expected him to love me and to teach me how to be a man, a husband, and a father. I expected him to nurture me spiritually, financially and professionally. The need for this kind of deep nurturing is real, but it is not realistic or fair for a son to expect so much of his father. The nature of humanity is to be incomplete and needy, but only God can ultimately fill that deep neediness. To a certain extent, I expected my father to be to me what only God is capable of being. Only one man, God's Son, has ever been capable of perfectly nurturing another man's development. Today, God's Holy Spirit ministers God the Father's healing and fulfillment through the support, encouragement, and nurturing of his people.

So every man will benefit if he has close relationships with many fathers or mentors who will minister God's healing love to him throughout his life. To grow, every man needs to know that other men will be available to him during times of crisis. To step into new areas, every man needs to know that other men have gone before him and are available to guide him into the unknown.

A Mentor for News Stage in Life

Mentors offer crucial help as men move into new stages of life. A man needs someone who is older to guide him toward his next steps of growth. He needs an older man to teach him what he needs to know in order to be successful. He needs a man to confront him with the harsh realities he would rather ignore. He needs someone to say the hard things that challenge him to deeper personal growth. He needs an older man who will express confidence in the man he is and will become.

In Tom Clancy's novel, *Clear and Present Danger*, I see an example of this kind of mentoring. There is a particularly moving exchange between two characters. Jack Ryan is being groomed to head the CIA. Admiral Greer, his longtime mentor, is dying of cancer. The two share this conversation during one of Ryan's visits to Greer at Bethesda Naval Hospital.

> He was barely a hundred pounds now, a scarecrow that had once been a man, a professional naval officer who'd commanded ships and led men in the service of their country. Fifty years of government service lay wasting away on the hospital bed. It was more than the death of a man. It was the death of an age, of a standard of behavior. Fifty years of experience and wisdom and judgment were slipping away. Jack took his seat next to the bed and waved the security officer out of the room.
> "Hey, boss."

His eyes opened.

Now what do I say? How are you feeling? There's something to say to a dying man!

"How was the trip, Jack?" the voice was weak.

"Belgium was okay. Everybody sends regards. Friday I got to brief Fowler, like you did the last time."

"What do you think of him?"

"I think he needs some help on foreign policy."

A smile: "So do I. Gives a nice speech, though."

"I didn't exactly hit it off with one of his aides, Elliot, the gal from Bennington...."

"Then you find her, and kiss and make up.... When are you going to learn to bend that stiff Irish neck of yours? Ask Basil sometime how much he likes the people he has to work for. Your duty is to serve the *country*, Jack, not just the people you happen to like." A blow from a professional boxer could not have stung worse.

"Yes, sir. You're right. I still have a lot to learn."

"Learn fast, boy. I haven't got many lessons left."

"Don't say that, Admiral." The line was delivered like the plea of a child.

"It's my time, Jack. Some men I served with died off Savo Island fifty years ago, or at Leyte, or lots of other parts of the ocean. I've been a lot luckier than they were, but it's my time. And it's your turn to take over for me. I want you to take my place, Jack."

"I do need some advice, Admiral."

"Columbia?"

"I could ask how you know, but I won't."

"When a man like Arthur Moore won't look you in the eye, you know that something is wrong. He was in here Saturday and he wouldn't look me in the eye."

"He lied to me today." Ryan explained on for five minutes, outlining what he knew, what he suspected, and what he feared.

"And you want to know what to do?" Greer asked.

"I could sure use a little guidance, Admiral."

"You don't need guidance, Jack. You're smart enough. You have all the contacts you need. And you know what's right."

"But what about—"

"Politics?..." Greer almost laughed. "Jack, you know, when you lay here like this, you know what you think about? You think about all the things you'd like another chance at, all the mistakes, all the people you might have treated better, and you thank God that it wasn't worse. Jack, you will never regret honesty, even if it hurts people. When they made you a Marine lieutenant you swore an oath before God. I understand why we do that now. It's a help, not a threat. It's something to remind you how important words are. Ideas are important. Principles are important. Words are important. Your word is the most important of all. Your word is who you are. That's the last lesson, Jack. You have to carry on from here." He paused, and Jack could see the pain coming through the heavy medications. "You have a family, Jack. Go home to them. Give 'em my love and tell them that I think their daddy is a pretty good guy, and they ought to be proud of him. Good night, Jack."[2]

All men should be so fortunate as to have an older man who will share with them in such an honest and caring manner. I enjoy reading all kinds of stories about men because the interaction and nature of male relationships in the stories. I think we can learn something about ourselves and our relationships by reading stories about other men—fiction or nonfiction. That is why I enjoy the stories of men and their relationships that are revealed through Scripture. These stories fascinate me and teach me so much.

To me, the story of David, the shepherd boy who loved God and became one of the greatest kings of Israel, is one of the most fascinating and revealing stories about male relationships. A number of events in David's life point toward a need for the kind of male friendships we have examined in this book. In the previous chapter, we looked at some of the initiatory events in David's life. Now let us look at the mentoring that took place in his life during a time of crisis.

Every Man Needs a Man to Run to in Crisis

For a time, things seemed to be going well in David's life. Samuel had anointed him king of Israel. The people honored him as their greatest war hero. He married Saul's daughter, and she loved him. And David had a loyal friend, Jonathan, Saul's son. The only problem was, Saul was insanely jealous of David. Saul's desire to kill David was so strong that even after he made a promise before God to let David live, he went back on his word. Notice how Scripture describes the situation:

> Saul listened to Jonathan and took this oath: "Assuredly as the Lord lives, David will not be put to death."
> So Jonathan called David and told him the whole conversation. He brought him to Saul, and David was with Saul as before (1 Samuel 19:6-7).

> But an evil spirit from the Lord came upon Saul as he was sitting in his house with his spear in his hand. While David was playing the harp, Saul tried to pin him to the wall with his spear, but David eluded him as Saul drove the spear into the wall. That night David made good his escape (1 Samuel 19:9-10).

Where did David go when he was forced to run for his life? He went straight to the older man who first initiated him into the world of men and into the world of kings. He went to Samuel. The Bible says, "When David had fled and made his escape, he went to Samuel at Ramah and told him all that Saul had done to him. Then he and Samuel went to Naioth and stayed there" (1 Samuel 19:18).

This is a powerful passage of Scripture. David was a young man in desperate trouble. Samuel was a great prophet who was recognized as the man of God during this time in Israel's history. He commanded great respect and honor throughout the nation. No man would challenge Samuel because God was with him.

David instinctively knew he would find safety by running toward a man of God! When David ran to Samuel, he did not go with an agenda of what he wanted Samuel to do for him. David went to him for the safety, strength, and connection with God that came from being with him. Imagine what it would be like to have a holy man, a spiritual leader, like Samuel to go to when you face frightening times.

When David and Samuel were together, David told him everything. He did not hold back. He related the entire story—everything Saul had done. After David shared what was on his mind and heart, he and Samuel went to a different place and spent time together. I think their example reveals some important aspects of mentoring during a time of crisis.

Support during a time of crisis is vital to a man's continued growth. A man who does not have someone to run to operates out of fear and is unable to take positive steps of growth. When I began my practice, I needed a man like Dr. Hawkins. Beginning a practice is a scary and worrisome thing for anyone. I did not know where my clients would come from or how I would pay my office expenses. I did not know if I'd have anything left to support my family. Even though I believed I was doing God's will, I was overwhelmed with fears and worries.

Just as David needed Samuel, every man today needs to talk to an older man who has made it through the struggles of life. Older men can have a deep sense of confidence and faith that God will indeed "cause all things to work together for good." During times of crisis, younger men need to be exposed to that strength of faith. They need to have an older man who can listen to their fears and respond. Smiles, gentle kidding, trusting prayer, a confident challenge, or encouraging advice all help to break the power of fear and help a man to go on.

The more a man shares what is on his heart, the more support he receives. I think it is wise to remember that David told Samuel everything. It is hard to tell another man everything. Pride is such a big obstacle. Most men learn early in life that reaching out for help is a sign of male weakness. More than anything else, men want to be viewed as real men. So it is easy for a man to feel embarrassed or shamed. Or he may fear that his mentor will condemn him if he honestly tells the whole story and completely unveils his feelings But if a man tells only part of the story, he will receive only part of the support his mentor can offer.

In crisis, a young man will gain the most when he seeks out a spiritually alive mentor. One aspect of Dr. Hawkins' mentoring that means the most to me is his solid, consistent spirituality. I have been calmed and relieved by the many times he has prayed for me. I have been blessed as he has shared exciting things he has discovered in his devotional life. I have been greatly comforted in knowing not only that he would be there to support me in a time of crisis, but that he would also direct me toward a deeper relationship with God.

Samuel's spiritual benefit to David, and to the nation of Israel, becomes clear as their story continues. After baring his heart to Samuel, David stayed with him. When Saul found out where David was, he sent men to capture him. Notice the impact of God's power that is conveyed through Samuel's spiritual leadership.

> But when they [Saul's men] saw a group of prophets prophesying, with Samuel standing there as their leader, the Spirit of God came upon Saul's men and they also prophesied. Saul was told about it, and he sent more men, and they prophesied too. Saul sent men a third time, and they also prophesied....
>
> So Saul went to Naioth at Ramah. But the Spirit of God came even upon him, and he walked along prophesying (1 Samuel 19:20-23).

Imagine this scene! Saul sent men to kill David. But the power of David's spiritual refuge overwhelmed those who came to destroy him! When faced with the decision to run away or to run to the wisdom, refuge, and strength of Samuel, David chose to run to his mentor. David was a mighty warrior, but he recognized his desperate need for support. I think David ran in the right direction!

When facing a crisis, the support of a group of men is tremendous. Another message I see in this passage of Scripture is the great potential of men who are united in the power of the Lord. The spiritual power of Samuel, the prophets, and David was so strong that it altered the course of Saul's messengers. Their mission was thwarted, and they were impacted by God's power. I think this is the most powerful men's support group recorded in Scripture.

It is hard to imagine what it means to have the support of a group of men unless you have shared that experienced. A man who feels protected and supported by a group of men is changed. The support of a group of men enables him to make right decisions and follow positive directions that he would otherwise be powerless to pursue. This is why the support concept in twelve-step groups such as Alcoholics Anonymous is so important. The ability to share with and receive support from a group of men enables a man to live one day at a time without succumbing to his addictions.

Even Saul, whose heart was hardened against David and against God, was touched by the scene at Naioth. What was happening there was so powerful that it stopped him in his tracks. God's Spirit broke through to Saul's heart, and he connected with God in a way that he had not experienced for many years. I do not think it was an accident that Saul made that connection with God while in the company of other men rather than when he was alone. I think this further illustrates how God works in the hearts of men through their relationships with one another.

Mentors Struggle Too

Although mentor relationships are necessary in a man's life, they are not without problems As Samuel Osherson points out, some of those problems stem from the father-son wound:

> The mentoring relationship suffers from the same deficiencies and stresses as other male relationships, particularly those of father and son. Notwithstanding its positive aspects, men often act out in the mentoring relationship unfinished conflicts with their own fathers and families.... Some mentors can be unconsciously destructive of their charges, and some mentees can demand an unattainable or inappropriate love from the mentor, which also interferes with their work.[3]

Rod, for example, worked in an insurance office. Soon after he began working there, Jim, the owner, took him under his wing. Rod was ecstatic. Jim was a Christian who appeared to be successful in his work, his faith, and his relationship with his family. Rod soaked up all the encouragement Jim could give. He modeled Jim's sales techniques and learned to provide not just good service, but excellent service. His client list grew rapidly and soon the parent company recognized Rod's accomplishments. Immediately after Rod received that recognition, Jim withdrew his support from him.

Rod was crushed. The little boy within him had thrived on Jim's praise and encouragement. They were the expressions of approval that Rod had not received from his father. Jim's own father-son wound had led him to become jealous of Rod's success and unable to recognize the valuable contribution Rod made to the company. Jim began to sabotage Rod's efforts by neglecting to give messages to Rod and by holding up vital information Rod needed to bring in new business. The deep needs of their respective father-son wounds led to an explosive termination of their relationship.

Things could have been different for Rod and Jim if they had been able to develop some awareness of their father-son wound and to deal with the deep feelings arising from it. Rod needed to recognize the source of his need for approval from Jim. Jim needed to become aware enough of his feelings that he could recognize his destructive response to Rod. But it isn't easy for a young man to find an older man who can mentor on a feeling level.

The feeling, nurturing potential of a mentor is often what draws the younger man to him. Yet many men have not dealt with their own father-son wound, and they are not equipped to fulfill the younger man's expectation of being a feeling mentor. Many mentors would rather pass on professional skills. They feel less able to nurture the development of a younger man's full masculine potential. As a result, much of the mentoring that takes place in our society focuses on a man's vocation, but ignores his heart.

One young physician describes his frustration with this type of mentoring:

> "I feel like there are mentors to show me how to be a surgeon in the old mold—completely dedicated to my work to the exclusion of everything else, inattentive to other people's feelings and needs, and willing to ruthlessly climb the ladder of success." The young physician stopped and thought for a moment, then plunged on:
> "But there aren't mentors, or at least I haven't found them, who can help me become a feeling, powerful man, as well as a physician."[4]

This lack of nurturing of the whole person is tragic, but understandable when we realize that most men (and therefore most mentors) also suffer from their own father-son wound. When a man has not delved into his own pain, he has no connection to his own feelings and certainly cannot connect with another man's feelings. It is only natural that a man who suffers a deficit of feelings within himself would only be able to mentor on a professional level.

It is a powerful thing to be mentored by a man who is connected to the deep feelings of his heart and can therefore touch the heart of a younger man. In my church there is such a man. Roger is an excellent businessman and a highly committed Christian. He has been in a serious recovery program for a number of years. He runs his own business in such a way that he can devote one day a week to the business concerns of the church. When I counsel young men who are struggling in business, I ask Roger to meet with them.

These young men always have the same reaction to him. They say they have never met a man who is as successful as he is yet listens to their concerns with such warmth and understanding. Roger is able to share with them about the facts of business life and discuss the hard choices and decisions they must make as business operators. He understands all aspects of their situation clearly and shares his options succinctly, yet conveys no blame or judgment that makes them feel naive or stupid. Roger has this tremendous gift because he has a good recovery going. He is a feeling man who is not afraid to express his love or commit himself to supporting and nurturing another man.

Dr. Hawkins is a similar mentor to physicians in training who do a rotation in family practice with him. (I expect the physician Osherson interviewed would love to have had such a doctor as Will mentor him.) The young physicians learn his skill because they watch him work. Many of them become enamored with his ability to get to the heart of a problem and quickly diagnose and treat it.

But Dr. Hawkins does more than teach how to treat illnesses. I've heard him share some of his fears and concerns as a physician. I've seen him educate his students about dysfunctional families and the relationship between those family issues and disease. As he teaches, he also helps them become aware of their own feelings and family issues. Consequently, a strong bond develops between him and his students. The physicians who train with Will complete more than a family practice rotation. They gain a significant relationship with an older man. Perhaps for the first time in their lives, the little boy (or girl) inside those physicians feel cared for and nurtured.

There is no substitute for a mentor who nurtures the whole man. I wish it were easy to find such men. Unfortunately, it is not. It takes work to find and develop relationships with mentors. Some of these men can be found in church. Others may be found in the workplace. Still others can be found in recovery groups. I encourage men to seek out and consider men they admire. Men who have a healthy focus on their emotional and spiritual growth make good mentors. Also, good mentors have a deep respect for other men, women, and children and they are not afraid of their feelings. I tell men to look for a man who touches them at a deep level and instills a desire to do their best in life. No man will be a perfect mentor, and many men can play a mentoring role as a man progresses through life.

Becoming a Mentor

Since there are no perfect mentors, they come in all types and ages. A man does not need to be eighty-five before he can become a mentor. In some ways a man is a mentor at whatever age he is. It is not so much a man's chronological age. It is his masculine maturity that makes him a mentor. A man who is willing to dip deeply into his soul and face the pain of his father-son wound has something to offer. A man who is emotionally connected with other men, has something to offer as a mentor. A man who seeks wholehearted and continued growth in relationship with his heavenly Father has something to offer as a mentor. And a man who is living out a solid recovery program has much to offer.

Becoming a mentor is a process that begins early in life and deepens as a man matures. My son Ben, for instance, was a kind of mentor to the younger boys in the neighborhood. These boys simply liked to hang around him. He was the big guy on the block and they look up to him. They couldn't wait for a chance to play basketball with him.

Ben, in turn, looked up to some college guys in the neighborhood. They came from a Christian family and were solid, feeling young men. They, too, came over to the house to play basketball. As they played, they'd talk about sports and girlfriends. By spending time with Ben, they affirmed him and fulfilled a mentoring role in his life.

Ben's youth group leader also played a mentoring role in Ben's life and the lives of a number of Ben's peers. Although he was only in his early twenties, this young man had much to pass on. He had a deep feeling for Christ. He modeled how to have a good time without drugs, alcohol, or sex. He enjoyed crazy things like riding an ice block down a hill or mildly disrupting the girls' youth group with water cannons. Still, he was able to share about the importance of staying true to Christ's teachings, even when it is difficult

As a man grows in his masculine strength, he has more and more to give to younger men as a mentor. He realizes he has learned something during his journey through life that is worth passing on. In primitive societies, the older men may devote 60 to 80 percent of their time to the work of initiating and mentoring the younger men. To be able to do so gives an older man a deep sense of purpose and meaning. He can take his last breath knowing that his life has counted for something. He can share his successes, his failures, his sources of pain, and his experiences of suffering and survival. He can keep a younger man from the mistakes he made. In a way, a mentor sifts through the ashes of his life to find the golden principles and lessons that remain. He polishes those treasures and passes them on to the generation that follows.

A Closer Look

Mentor—A male mentor nurtures a younger man in his masculine development. Mentors impart their values, experience, and life to another man. A mentor is a more senior, usually older, person in the world. He serves a transitional function for the young man, helping him to become established in the adult world of men. He also imparts his own special values and beliefs. The mentor serves very important, healthy functions in helping the younger man mature into adulthood. More than one mentor is needed in a man's growth and transition through the stages of life. And every area of a man's life can benefit from the support of a mentor.

Mentee—A mentee is the younger man who is mentored. Although he is on the receiving end of a mentoring relationship, the mentee also provides a benefit to the mentor. Indeed, many men find that the mentoring relationship allows them to heal some of the wounds of parenting. Some men see their mentees as "surrogate sons."

Personal Reflection

1. What experience have you had with a mentor in business or personal life? How did the mentor help you? How did he make you feel?

2. Who are the men who impacted your development in school, career, and family life? Any special teachers, professors, bosses, older men?

3. What transitions in your life have been most difficult for you to manage? In what ways could a mentor have helped?

4. Can you recall a crisis in your life when you reached out to an older man for help? What was your experience?

5. What is most troubling experience you have had to face in your life? What did you discover about yourself or God or life that could help another man?

NOTES:

CHAPTER 11

The Healing Power
of Male Friendships

Most men are experts at maintaining superficial relationships. They may have social connections with other men at work. They may enjoy a great time with their buddies on softball, bowling, or basketball teams. They may even spend an amazing amount of time talking with neighbors about lawn fertilizer. It is rare, however, for male relationships to offer any degree of emotional or spiritual support that will help a man heal from his deepest wounds and challenge him to keep growing and developing as a man

Male conversations usually focus on talk about work, sports, interest rates, and politics rather than on the deeper issues of life that truly trouble a man. I am amazed how a man can talk pleasantly about superficial football trivia while he silently suffers internal turmoil and distress. He may be full inner conflicts—thoughts of an affair, memories of past abuse, worries about his drinking, or struggles with an addiction to pornography or prostitutes. He may be so depressed that he barely makes it out of bed in the morning. He may feel angry or distant toward God. But most men would not dare share such feelings with another man. Most men have not had a close friend since high school, college, or the service.

This is truly a tragedy. According to some researchers, the lack of intimate male friendships is a major social problem in our society. It significantly affects a man's psychological and physical health.[1] Men need friends with whom they can share everything. They need friends who will stand by them and offer support and strength in times of trouble. Every man needs a trustworthy friend who knows everything there is to know about him. These intimate, honest and vulnerable masculine relationships are necessary if men are to heal from their father-son wound and grow into mature manhood.

Rabbi Baal Shem Tov is credited with a saying that describes the kind of caring, committed, strong friendships every man needs: "To pull a friend out of the mire, don't hesitate to get dirty."[2] A man who has a friend like this is fortunate indeed, but few men today are blessed with the treasure of a true friend. Let us take a close look at a deep male friendship that is recorded in scripture the friendship between Jonathan and David.

A Bond Between Warriors

At the time David and Jonathan met, they had already proven themselves to be great warriors. No soft, palace wimps, they were identified as the outstanding war heroes of Israel. By anyone's standards they had earned their status as real men.

Jonathan was the son of the king of Israel, a protector of the nation. At one time he commanded one-third of Israel's army. His courage and strength in battle were well known, as was his ability to inspire courage and loyalty in others. While the army of Israel was in hiding, afraid to do battle against the Philistines, Jonathan and his armor-bearer launched an attack against a Philistine outpost. It was a feat not even Rambo could pull off! Notice the courage, confidence, and spiritual conviction of their adventure:

> On each side of the pass that Jonathan intended to cross to reach the Philistine outpost was a cliff; one was called Bozez, and the other Seneh. One cliff stood to the north toward Micmash, the other to the south toward Geba.
>
> Jonathan said to his young armor-bearer, "Come, let's go over to the outpost of those uncircumcised fellows. Perhaps the LORD will act in our behalf. Nothing can hinder the LORD from saving, whether by many or by few."
>
> "Do all that you have in mind," his armor-bearer said. "Go ahead; I am with you heart and soul."
>
> Jonathan said, "Come, then; we will cross over toward the men and let them see us. If they say to us, 'Wait there until we come to you,' we will stay where we are and not go up to them.

But if they say, 'Come up to us,' we will climb up, because that will be our sign that the LORD has given them into our hands."

So both of them showed themselves to the Philistine outpost. "Look!" said the Philistines. "The Hebrews are crawling out of the holes they were hiding in." The men of the outpost shouted to Jonathan and his armor-bearer, "Come up to us and we'll teach you a lesson."

So Jonathan said to his armor-bearer, "Climb up after me; the LORD has given them into the hand of Israel."

Jonathan climbed up, using his hands and feet, with his armor-bearer right behind him. The Philistines fell before Jonathan, and his armor-bearer followed and killed behind him (1 Samuel 14:3-13).

What a leader Jonathan is! Led by the conviction that God would direct their actions, Jonathan and his armor-bearer embarked on what appeared to be a suicide mission. Without a moment's hesitation, the two men took a step of incredible courage and killed more than twenty Philistines. Then God sent a panic through the whole Philistine army, and Israel was delivered from their enemies that day.

Afterward, when Saul was ready to put Jonathan to death for disobeying an order that Jonathan had never heard, the men of Israel said the following:

But the men said to Saul, "Should Jonathan die—he who has brought about this great deliverance in Israel? Never! As surely as the LORD lives, not a hair of his head will fall to the ground, for he did this today with God's help." So the men rescued Jonathan, and he was not put to death (1 Samuel 14:45).

Jonathan was so well respected that the army of Israel was willing to stand against their king in order to protect him!

David, although not from the royal family, had been chosen by God to be king of Israel after Saul. Beginning with his contest against the giant Goliath, David, too, had earned a reputation as one of Israel's greatest warriors.

David did not set out to be a great warrior. His first visit to a battlefield was in response to his father's instruction to deliver food to his older brothers and to find out how they were doing. As soon as David arrived on the scene, he was caught up in the tension, challenge, fear, and excitement of battle:

> He reached the camp as the army was going out to its battle positions, shouting the war cry. Israel and the Philistines were drawing up their lines facing each other. David left his things with the keeper of supplies, ran to the battle lines and greeted his brothers. As he was talking with them, Goliath, the Philistine champion from Gath, stepped out from his lines and shouted his usual defiance, and David heard it. When the Israelites saw the man, they all ran from him in great fear (1 Samuel 17:20-24).

Imagine what it was like for David, a seventeen-year-old shepherd![3] The Israelite army had lived with the tension of maintaining a state of battle readiness for quite some time. Goliath had been issuing his defiant challenge every day for forty days. Daily his words chilled the hearts of the weary Israelites, and they ran from him in fear.

Their fear was understandable. Goliath was nine feet, nine inches tall—definitely qualifying for any NBA team He was a strong warrior, feared even by the Philistines. He wore a bronze helmet and suit of armor that weighed 125 pounds. The tip of his spear weighed 15 pounds.[4] Not even Saul, the king of Israel, would stand against him in battle.

David was different. At that time in his life, he had a close relationship with God. He probably spent many otherwise lonely hours in communion with God, sharing everything in his heart with his heavenly Father and connecting with his sure reply. He was appalled that any man, giant or not, would defy the "armies of the living God." On the basis of his spiritual conviction, David decided to fight Goliath.

David's decision to take on the giant's challenge showed great courage, but his decision to fight without armor, without the traditional protection, and weapons of war is astounding! With a deep spiritual conviction similar to the kind Jonathan had shown in attacking the Philistine outpost, David moved onto the battlefield against Goliath. Just as Jonathan did, he faced the taunts of his enemy and conquered:

> Then he took his staff in his hand, chose five smooth stones from the stream, put them in the pouch of his shepherd's bag and, with his sling in his hand, approached the Philistine.
>
> Meanwhile, the Philistine, with his shield bearer in front of him, kept coming closer to David. He looked David over and saw that he was only a boy, ruddy and handsome, and he despised him. He said to David, "Am I a dog, that you come at me with sticks?" And the Philistine cursed David by his gods. "Come here," he said, "and I'll give your flesh to the birds of the air and the beasts of the field!"
>
> David said to the Philistine, "You come against me with sword and spear and javelin, but I come against you in the name of the LORD Almighty, the God of the armies of Israel, whom you have defied. This day the LORD will hand you over to me, and I'll strike you down and cut off your head. Today I will give the carcasses of the Philistine army to the birds of the air and the beasts of the earth, and the whole world will know that there is a God in Israel. All those gathered here will know that it is not by sword or spear that the LORD saves; for the battle is the Lord's, and he will give all of you into our hands."
>
> As the Philistine moved closer to attack him, David ran quickly toward the battle line to meet him. Reaching into his bag and taking out a stone, he slung it and struck the Philistine on the forehead. The stone sank into his forehead, and he fell facedown on the ground.
>
> So David triumphed over the Philistine with a sling and a stone; without a sword in his hand he struck down the Philistine and killed him (1 Samuel 17:40-50).

What a warrior! David's action led to a great victory for Israel. The people were overjoyed at their delivery from the Philistines' oppression and credited David with the victory. The women danced in the streets, singing, "Saul has slain his thousands, and David his tens of thousands." Immediately after David killed Goliath, Saul spoke with David. Jonathan apparently was nearby, listening, for Scripture says:

> After David had finished talking with Saul, Jonathan became one in spirit with David.... And Jonathan made a covenant

with David because he loved him as himself Jonathan took off the robe he was wearing and gave it to David, along with his tunic, and even his sword, his bow and his belt (1 Samuel 18:1-4).

This marked the beginning of the covenant friendship between Jonathan and David.

The Gift of Covenant Friendship

The relationship between Jonathan and David was no casual acquaintance. It was a deep, committed love relationship between powerful men. In fact, Scripture says more than once that Jonathan loved David as he loved himself.

The depth of their commitment to each other was dramatically illustrated by Jonathan's gifts to David, which symbolized the deep level of respect, humility, trust, and loyalty inherent in their relationship. Jonathan took off the items of clothing that symbolized his royal status as son of the king of Israel and gave them to David. He literally handed over the outward evidence of his status in the world to his friend. This is not something a man does lightly. It is even more amazing that Jonathan also gave David his weapons, his means of defense.

Even today men have a strong attachment to their weapons. Men who own guns seem to have no shortage of stories and praises to relate about their favorite pistols, rifles, or shotguns. Boys rarely forget the first knife or .22 rifle they receive. When a boy receives such a gift, he feels as if he has gained recognition that he is more than just a boy. When he carries a knife around in his pocket or walks through the woods or fields with his rifle, he feels as if he belongs in the world of men. He imagines himself as a man, fighting off bears, mountain lions, and bad guys with the weapons in his hands. Imagine how much stronger a great warrior's attachment to his weapons would be!

This interaction between Jonathan and David is beautiful. Jonathan's gifts communicate his deep commitment to David, and David accepts these symbols of commitment without protest. He does not say, "Oh, Jonathan, you shouldn't do this. This sword is too valuable to give to me." It is not easy for a man to accept a gift of such depth from another man. Yet the gift of covenant friendship is a gift all men need in their lives.

I experienced such a friendship when I was in my late twenties. I was worked at a mental health center in conjunction with a community group home for the developmentally disabled. I met Hal and Marion Lynch, whose youngest daughter had Down's Syndrome. Through our interaction at planning meetings, public hearings, and the like, we developed a friendship.

Hal, a successful banker, exemplified the values of hard work, honesty, and loyalty to God, his wife, his children, and his community. I often met with Hal and Marion over lunch to discuss plans for the group home. I usually met them at the bank, then we would walk down the street to a small cafe. A curious thing happened to us almost every time we walked a few steps outside the bank. Marion would stop to say hello to someone she knew, and a few steps further on Hal would walk across the street to chat with someone he saw. Invariably we walked down the street in a crisscross fashion. We eventually ended up at the cafe at about the same time! I will always remember how Hal and Marion warmly greeted each person they met and how they genuinely cared about what was happening in the lives of others. In Hal I saw a deeply caring and generous man who supported the people in his community in tangible ways, regardless of their status or depth of need. He was not afraid to commit himself and his resources to others.

I was not easy for me to tell Hal about my decision to move my family to California where I could go back to school to earn my doctorate. I was not afraid of his response, but it was hard to face the loss of moving away from such a good man and dear friend. When Hal learned that I was making the move without any assurance that I would have a job, he reached into his pocket and gave me five $100 bills. He said, "Make sure, when you get to California and move into your house, that you and Karen use this money to buy something nice for yourselves." I took the money and immediately wanted to give it back because I did not feel worthy of such a gift. Hal continued, "And I want you to know that if you ever need money while you are in school, you just call us. We'll send it to you."

When Hall said this to me, I began to cry. The little boy within me had never received a gift quite like this one—a generous gift with no strings attached. Plus he committed to help me out whenever I needed it. I knew from experience that when Hal made a commitment, you could take it to the bank.

I needed money several times during graduate school and whenever I asked, Hal quickly sent it to me. When times were tough, it felt good to know that another man had such deep love and confidence in me that he was willing to verbally and materially support me whenever I needed it. When I got out of school, I paid Hal back first—not because he asked me to, but because I so appreciated his trust and commitment.

I have often wondered if what I felt in my relationship with Hal is similar to what David felt in his friendship with Jonathan. Jonathan was certainly a friend who was not afraid to commit himself wholeheartedly—he held nothing back. Their friendship was more than a happy camaraderie that overflowed in the ecstatic moments of victory. David knew that when Jonathan made a commitment to him, he would come through.

As their lives unfolded, David and Jonathan experienced situations that tested their commitment to one another and stretched the depths of their relationship. Their response to these difficult and painful circumstances shows how a covenant relationship with another man directs a man in his walk with God, enables him to share and resolve his deepest feelings and fears, supports him during his darkest hours, and develops his character. Let us consider the qualities of their friendship that promote healing for a man's soul and encourage his masculine growth.

Covenant Friends Are Loyal and Trustworthy

After their covenant of friendship was established, David and Jonathan continued to be warriors of Israel, fighting against the Philistines. David, particularly, met with great success. The people loved and praised him. As David's popularity grew, King Saul became increasingly afraid of him. Saul did everything he could to thwart David's efforts and even tried to kill him.

David was in a difficult position. He had done nothing but serve his king and country as best he could. Yet he was both loved and hated. He was on an emotional roller coaster. First, he was viewed as special by the king, and later viewed as an enemy. Then he was highly esteemed by the people, but pursued by a king who literally wanted to pin him to the wall. Perhaps David even wondered if his relationship with Jonathan, Saul's son, would survive this threat. If so, he did not have to worry, for Jonathan was a man of deep integrity and unfailing loyalty. Notice how courageously he intervened on David's behalf:

> Saul told his son Jonathan and all the attendants to kill David. But Jonathan was very fond of David and warned him, "My father Saul is looking for a chance to kill you. Be on your guard tomorrow morning; go into hiding and stay there. I will go out and stand with my father in the field where you are. I'll speak to him about you and will tell you what I find out."
>
> Jonathan spoke well of David to Saul his father and said to him, "Let not the king do wrong to his servant David; he has not wronged you, and what he has done has benefited you greatly. He took his life in his hands when he killed the Philistine. The LORD won a great victory for all Israel, and you saw it and were glad. Why then would you do wrong to an innocent man like David by killing him for no reason?"
>
> Saul listened to Jonathan and took this oath: "As surely as the LORD lives, David will not be put to death."
>
> So Jonathan called David and told him the whole conversation. He brought him to Saul, and David was with Saul as before (1 Samuel 19:1-7).

Who could ask for a more courageous friend than Jonathan? There is no doubt about where his loyalty resides. He is willing to risk his own reputation and safety in order to protect his friend. Saul's hatred of David was growing, and his behavior was becoming increasingly manipulative, violent, and unpredictable. There was no guarantee that Saul would respond positively when Jonathan spoke well of David. In fact, Jonathan's actions exposed him to real personal risk.

The character traits of loyalty and trustworthiness seem almost endangered among men today. As families continue to be destroyed by dysfunctional behavior and a culture that has lost its basic, biblical values, loyal and trustworthy men become harder and harder to find. The problems and addictions of each successive generation produce fewer men who model these important qualities of character for the younger men. Yet men of all ages hunger for relationships with men who live by these values, no matter what the cost.

An incident in pastor Stuart Briscoe's life illustrates this well. After he got out of the service, Stuart took a job in a bank. He worked hard and took on additional responsibilities, and soon one of the bank executives noticed him. This particular executive had a reputation for periodic rages and unreasonable demands. Bank employees dreaded interaction with him and hoped they would never have to work for him. This executive became Stuart's new boss.

Stuart had not been on the job long when he received a call for his boss. When Stuart conveyed the message, his boss told him to tell the customer he was not in. Stuart realized he was being asked to lie. So he mustered his courage, fully realizing that he might be yelled at and fired, and confronted his boss. "If I agree to lie for you now," he said, "you will never know if you can really trust me. Wouldn't you like to have one employee who you know will not lie for you—and most likely will not lie to you?"

Stuart's response stopped his boss in his tracks. He looked at Stuart for a moment, then agreed to take the call. His boss realized that he was dealing with a man of integrity and principle a man who was loyal and trustworthy.

We need many such men in our world today. Men who are loyal and trustworthy make good friends. True friendship cannot exist apart from these characteristics. A man who wants to grow in the character traits of loyalty, integrity, and trustworthiness needs to seek out relationships with such men. Covenant friendship builds on these character traits and enables men to continue maturing in these areas throughout their lives.

Covenant Friends Work Through Their Conflicts

Loyalty and trust are fundamental parts of true friendship. The trying circumstances of life may at times put them to the test. As friends face these circumstances together, the depth of their loyalty and trust is revealed. If the friendship is true, friends learn that they can safely share their deepest emotions, even their most intense frustrations and greatest fears. They know they can work through whatever conflicts may arise. This happened to David and Jonathan not long after Jonathan intervened to save David from Saul.

For a time life seemed to return to normal and go well for David. He continued to battle the Philistines when necessary and spent time at home playing the harp for Saul. But life did not give David much breathing room. Suddenly his life turned upside down again:

> But an evil spirit from the Lord came upon Saul as he was sitting in his house with his spear in his hand. While David was playing the harp, Saul tried to pin him to the wall with his spear, but David eluded him as Saul drove the spear into the wall. That night David made good his escape. (1 Samuel 19:8-10).

Picture David calmly playing music of praise before the king when suddenly Saul tries to skewer him! From this point on, David does not take any chances. His wife, Michal (Saul's daughter), helps him escape. After spending time with Samuel, his spiritual mentor, David goes straight to Jonathan, his friend.

This is no casual, let's-talk-about-the-good-old-days social visit. David is frustrated, angry, and frightened. He meets Jonathan and says, "What have I done? What is my crime? How have I wronged your father, that he is trying to take my life?" (1 Samuel 20:1).

Apparently Saul's recent attempt on David's life is news to Jonathan. "Never!" Jonathan replied. "You are not going to die! Look, my father doesn't do anything, great or small, without confiding in me. Why would he hide this from me? It's not so!" (1 Samuel 20:2).

It is risky to share such deep and painful feelings. When men share what is truly in their hearts, they may be misunderstood and conflict may arise in their relationship. That is what happened during this interaction between David and Jonathan. David tells Jonathan that Saul tried to kill him. Jonathan says that it cannot be true. Conflict like this tests a friendship. No one quite knows how the conflict will be resolved.

But remember that David and Jonathan shared a sacred covenant. Their friendship was built on more than their feelings toward one another. It was built on a deep commitment that was made before God and sealed by Jonathan's symbolic gifts to David. Instead of brushing off the problem and distancing themselves from one another, David and Jonathan go deeper and deal with the tough reality of life. Notice how David responds to Jonathan's denial:

> But David took an oath and said, "Your father knows very well that I have found favor in your eyes, and he has said to himself, 'Jonathan must not know this or he will be grieved.' Yet as surely as the Lord lives and as you live, there is only a step between me and death" (1 Samuel 20:3).

David does not mince any words here. He reveals the hard truth in a way that Jonathan cannot deny. David makes his statement under oath, and Jonathan knows that David would never lie under these circumstances. David affirms Jonathan's loyalty by telling him that the truth has been kept from him because of his unfailing friendship with David. David is not afraid to tell Jonathan the truth about Saul, even though his words must have been a painful reminder to Jonathan of the depth of his wound with his father Saul. David also is not afraid to admit to his friend that he is as good as dead

David's words must have touched Jonathan deeply, for his reply was simple: "Whatever you want me to do, I'll do for you" (1 Samuel 20:4).

Vulnerability had been a characteristic of this relationship from the beginning. At the outset, when Jonathan gave his weapons to David, he was completely defenseless and vulnerable. David possessed the means of Jonathan's protection and could have killed him with his own sword. When his life was threatened by his friend's father, David came to Jonathan and, by honestly exposing everything in his heart, became vulnerable to Jonathan. David's fate was now in Jonathan's hands, and his friend responded by honoring that trust. He committed himself to do whatever was necessary to protect David

This type of complete vulnerability is essential in a covenant friendship between men. Vulnerability includes a willingness to talk about and deal with dark aspects of life. It also means being honest enough to share and accept one another's deepest fears. Vulnerability and trust are necessary if men are to work through conflicts in their relationships. If one man holds back or is not trustworthy, the relationship is not safe. When men have a deep commitment to one another and are vulnerable enough to be truly honest with one another, healing can take place in their lives.

Covenant Friends Share and Work through Their Deepest Feelings

After his time with Samuel, David went to Jonathan to share what was happening and to let off some steam. He needed Jonathan to hear him out, to give him some perspective on what was happening in his life. David knew he had done nothing but good in all of his dealings with Saul. He had put his life on the line numerous times as he served his king, God, and country. Yet when David least expected it, Saul had attacked him.

In one way or another, these kinds of things happen in the lives of many men. It is not unusual for a man to be a victim of unjust anger from his boss, wife, parents or others. It is not unusual for unpredictable situations to generate fear or worry deep in a man's heart when feelings of anger, fear, frustration, worry, resentment, sadness, and hurt well up in a man, he needs a friend (or group of friends) with whom he can share those feelings It is not good for a man to be alone with those feelings. Just as David needed to share his feelings with Jonathan, men today need to share their feelings with one another.

Consider the situation Andy faced because he worked for a man who was an alcoholic. Whenever this man drank too much, everyone in the office was on pins and needles. The boss's expectations were unreasonable. His constant demands created an atmosphere of chronic tension. Minor mistakes resulted in major blowups. Andy lived with nearly constant stomach pain and tension headaches. By the time he arrived home at night, after nearly ten hours of tension and anxiety, his wife and family faced a six-foot bundle of raw nerves. He was like a coiled spring, ready to explode if he had to deal with any more tension.

One night, as he walked into the house, his eight-year-old son greeted him with the words, "Daddy, can you fix my bike? The chain fell off."

Andy turned toward him and yelled, "Do you expect me to fix everything around here?"

No sooner were the words out of his mouth than Andy realized he had brought the monster from work home with him. With horror he saw tears well up in his son's eyes. Since Andy had begun to realize how the little boy within him was being wounded at work, he could see how he had wounded his son. Tears filled his own eyes. He knelt down, held his son close, and told him he was sorry. Then he took his son's hand and together they walked into the garage to fix the bike.

When a man locks up his deep feelings of hurt, the people closest to him, usually his wife and children, become the unfortunate victims of the pain he carries inside. If a man truly desires to be a real man—the kind of husband and father his family needs— he has to be able to share with another man the deep, hurtful feelings he carries inside. Like David, men today need a safe place where they can share their feelings of woundedness and know that they are heard. Like David and Jonathan, men today need to wrestle through their feelings with another man.

David openly and directly expressed his raw emotions of frustration, fear, anger, and injustice. Jonathan listened to him and offered a comforting perspective. Unfortunately, Jonathan's perspective was flawed. David came back at him with a jarring dose of reality. David's words brought his friend back on track, forcing him to realize that assurances could do nothing to lessen the threat against David's life. Only then were Jonathan and David ready to deal with the situation at hand. Together they planned a solution that they could not have accomplished on their own.

This is a wonderful example of the deep healing of the masculine soul that can take place through covenant friendship. There is no doubt in my mind that men today need these kinds of relationships. These relationships can develop between friends or between men in a twelve-step support group. The important thing is that covenant relationships enable men to share their deep feelings. They challenge men to stay focused on reality rather than drifting off into their fantasies. They help men deal in positive ways with whatever crises they may face. Let us see where the vulnerability and commitment between Jonathan and David takes them.

Covenant Friends Offer Unwavering Support

When Jonathan told David that he would do whatever David wanted him to do, he meant *anything*. His commitment came from the depths of his soul. They both knew his commitment could be costly. After all, Jonathan's father had tried to kill David. Once Jonathan reaffirmed their commitment, David presented his immediate problem and plan to him:

> So David said, "Look, tomorrow is the New Moon festival, and I am supposed to dine with the king; but let me go and hide in the field until the evening of the day after tomorrow. If your father misses me at all, tell him, 'David earnestly asked my permission to hurry to Bethlehem, his hometown, because an annual sacrifice is being made there for his whole clan.' If he says, 'Very well,' then your servant is safe. But if he loses his temper, you can be sure that he is determined to harm me" (1 Samuel 20:5-7).

David was in a precarious position. Even with their commitment to one another, it was not easy these friends to deal with the strong feelings that arose between than. They had to continue to probe one another, expressing their feelings to see how they were being received. After presenting his plan, David said:

> "As for you, show kindness to your servant, for you have brought him into a covenant with you before the LORD. If I am guilty, then kill me yourself! Why hand me over to your father?"
>
> "Never!" Jonathan said. "If I had the least inkling that my father was determined to harm you, wouldn't I tell you?"
>
> David asked, "Who will tell me if your father answers you harshly?" (1 Samuel 20:8-10).

David knows the pressure Jonathan will be under to carry out this plan. He knows the risk of being betrayed by his friend and the risk Jonathan faces in his relationship with Saul. This is not an easy friendship for them to continue. It could lead to death for one or both of them. In the face of imminent danger, they reach down deep into the care of their emotions and spiritual commitment and reaffirm their relationship before God:

> Then Jonathan said to David: "By the LORD, the God of Israel, I will surely sound out my father by this time the day after tomorrow! If he is favorably disposed toward you, will I not send you word and let you know? But if my father is inclined to harm you, may the LORD deal with me, be it ever so severely, if I do not let you know and send you away safely. May the LORD be with you as he has been with my father. But show me unfailing kindness like that of the LORD as long as I live, so that I may not be killed, and do not ever cut off your kindness from my family—not even when the LORD has cut off every one of David's enemies from the face of the earth."

> So Jonathan made a covenant with the house of David, saying, "May the LORD call David's enemies to account." And Jonathan had David reaffirm his oath out of love for him, because he loved him as he loved himself (1 Samuel 20:12-17).

Imagine what it would mean to have a relationship like this! Saul is the most powerful man in Israel. Men go into action at his command, whether it be to play music, go to war, eat dinner, or kill someone. As Saul becomes more intent on killing David, Jonathan's position becomes increasingly risky. Yet Jonathan does not withdraw from David for his own safety. He sticks right in there with him, no matter how tough it gets.

In keeping with the precarious situation they face, both men reaffirm their commitment to one another. This is an important thing for men to do during trying times. When a man deals with great pain, shameful feelings, or great risk, he needs to know if his friend is still with him. If a man senses that his friend's commitment is wavering, the issue needs to be addressed directly and honestly. There is no room for guesswork in a crisis. A man needs to know if his friend will hang in with him or bail out.

This need to reaffirm one's commitment is not a question of a man's integrity or honor. There was no doubt about the integrity or honesty of Jonathan or David. Still, they needed to verify the depth of their commitment as the situation became more serious. When men deal with serious situations, one of them may reach a point where he can risk no more. The fear of abandonment or rejection is something that all men fear. Covenant friends need to ask where they stand and continue deepening their commitment as their relationship grows. That is what Jonathan and David did as they faced the crisis before them.

Covenant Friends Watch Out for One Another — Whatever the Risk

The first night of the New Moon festival passed without incident. Saul noticed that David was absent, but said nothing. But when David was absent the second night, the crisis blew wide open. Saul asked Jonathan why David was not there, and Jonathan replied exactly as David had asked him to. The worst scenario that David and Jonathan had imagined followed:

> Saul's anger flared up at Jonathan and he said to him, "You son of a perverse and rebellious woman! Don't I know that you have sided with the son of Jesse to your own shame and to the shame of the mother who bore you? As long as the son of Jesse lives on this earth, neither you nor your kingdom will be established. Now send and bring him to me, for he must die!"
>
> "Why should he be put to death? What has he done?" Jonathan asked his father (1 Samuel 20:30-32).

Every man needs a friend like Jonathan who is willing to go to the wall for him. Once again, Jonathan tried to bring Saul back to reality with the truth about David's goodness. He boldly stood up against his father's unrighteous hatred, in firm opposition to what was wrong, no matter what the price. He nearly paid for this loyalty with his life.

Every man needs other men in his life who will stand by him and watch his back. Men who are in combat together work as a unit, each watching out for the other. When a man goes into battle, it means a lot to know that He can count on his buddies when the going gets tough. Men need this kind of support, not only in battle but in everyday life.

Al, for example, experienced several years of incredible success in his job. His work greatly benefited the corporation he worked for, but he did not know that his division manager felt threatened by his success. Al's close friend, Ted, however, had heard Al's division manager make derogatory comments about Al's work to the company president. It was apparent to Ted that the division manager was setting Al up to be fired. Ted told Al all that he had heard and suspected.

Al understood what was at stake and began sending the company president duplicate copies of the reports he was sending to his division manager. Before long, the company president recognized the division manager's game and fired him. The president then promoted Al to division manager. Al was fortunate to have a friend who let him know he was about to be attacked.

A man's enemies are not always external. Jim cared deeply for Ray. They had known each other for years and had shared about the ups and downs of business and family life with each other many times. But one thing about Ray bothered Jim. He had observed that Ray's social use of alcohol had become a regular part of his daily life. Jim thought he recognized several symptoms of alcoholism in Ray's behavior. Still, Jim did not know what if anything, he should say to his friend.

Jim's course of action became clear to him at a party in his home. Jim noticed a strong smell of alcohol on Ray's breath when he first arrived. As the evening progressed, Ray was a little louder than usual. A couple of times his behavior was out of control, causing others at the party to feel uncomfortable. As Jim thought about what he had seen in Ray's behavior that evening and over the past few years, he became certain that Ray was an alcoholic. Jim also connected this alcoholism to what had been happening in Ray's business. Although generally a solid businessman, Ray had made a series of bad decisions during the past year. His decisions seemed out of character and put his business in financial jeopardy. In light of this evidence, Jim decided he had to confront his friend.

It was not easy for Jim to talk to his friend about his concerns. To do so would mean risking many years of friendship. But as Ray's friend, he knew he could not sit back and watch Ray's health decline, his marriage deteriorate, and his business fail. Ray listened quietly as Jim explained what he had observed. When Jim was finished, Ray tearfully acknowledged that he could not control his drinking and did not know what to do. With Jim's support, Ray took positive steps to get help for his problem. By bringing this difficult issue out in the open, Jim went to the wall for his friend.

Jim was fortunate that his efforts to be a friend no matter what were as painless as they turned out to be. Jonathan was not as fortunate. The incident with Saul at the New Moon festival deeply wounded Jonathan. His worst nightmare had come true: his own father had shamed him in public and then tried to kill him. Jonathan did not eat for the remainder of the day. Despite his personal pain, scripture says that Jonathan's reason for fasting was because of his grief at his father's shameful treatment of David.

Covenant Friends Keep Confidences

What an incredible friend Jonathan had proven himself to be. He risked his life for his friend. Early the next morning, he set out to keep his commitment to reveal the bad news to David. This part of the story exposes another quality essential in a covenant relationship—absolute confidentiality:

> In the morning Jonathan went out to the field for his meeting with David. He had a small boy with him, and he said to the boy, "Run and find the arrows I shoot." As the boy ran, he shot an arrow beyond him. When the boy came to the place where Jonathan's arrow had fallen, Jonathan called out after him, "Isn't the arrow beyond you?" Then he shouted, "Hurry! Go quickly! Don't stop!" The boy picked up the arrow and returned to his master. (The boy knew nothing of all this; only Jonathan and David knew.) Then Jonathan gave his weapons to the boy and said, "Go, carry them back to town" (1 Samuel 20:35-40).

It would have been easy for Jonathan to tell Saul everything he knew in order to save his own neck. The situation was tense enough that Jonathan would have felt relieved if he had shared some of the emotional burden he carried with another man, but he did not. Certainly the boy who chased arrows for Jonathan would have been intrigued if Jonathan had revealed the true intent of their excursion, but Jonathan told him nothing.

Scripture clearly states that only Jonathan and David knew of their pact to verify Saul's intentions and protect David's life. Their words were simple, but they say much about the depth of trust and strength between these two great men. It was absolutely essential that what David and Jonathan shared between them stayed between them.

Keeping another man's confidence is a sacred part of masculine friendship. The ability to keep a confidence inspires trust and trust enables a man to share whatever it is that keeps him in bondage so that he may heal. A man cannot risk sharing what is in his heart unless he has the assurance that what he says will be kept in confidence. It is no small matter for a man to share deep feelings, dark secrets and hidden failures. When a man takes the risk to do so, he should not have to worry whether what he says will become common knowledge in his church, workplace, or community.

Sadly, most men today have never experienced this level of trust in their relationships with other men. This is one reason I recommend that men who are in recovery become involved in a twelve-step support group. Confidentiality is an essential element in twelve-step meetings such as Alcoholics Anonymous and Overcomers Outreach. At the beginning of every meeting, those who attend affirm that what is said in the meeting stays in the meeting. Within the safety of a commitment to confidentiality, whether within a twelve-step group or within a covenant friendship, a man can safely share what is on his heart.

Jonathan and David shared a commitment to confidentiality, so they felt completely safe with one another. They could tell each other anything. Within the safety of their relationship, they were free to expose the deepest feelings of their hearts.

Covenant Friends Touch One Another on a Deep Level

After Jonathan gave David the promised signal, he sent the boy who was with him back to town. David had been watching them all along and when Jonathan was alone, David came out to meet him. Notice what scripture reveals about their friendship in their last meeting:

> After the boy had gone, David got up from the south side of the stone and bowed down before Jonathan three times, with his face to the ground. Then they kissed each other and wept together—but David wept the most.
>
> Jonathan said to David, "Go in peace, for we have sworn friendship with each other in the name of the LORD, saying, 'The LORD is witness between you and me, and between your descendants and my descendants forever.'" Then David left, and Jonathan went back to the town (1 Samuel 20:41-42).

Realizing that they might never see one another again, David and Jonathan make no attempt to hide their feelings. Their loss is almost beyond words, so they hold each other and cry. It is no secret that these two great warriors meant much to each other.

It is very healing to let these feelings out and to share them with another man. One of the moments in my life that I prize the most is a time when my father opened up and shared his deep feelings with me. I was a teenager at the time and had awakened earlier than usual. As I walked from the house to the barn to do the milking, it seemed important that I get to the barn as quickly as I could. This was an unusual feeling for me because, as a teenager, I was often less than enthusiastic about morning milking. As I walked through the barn door, I saw Dad leaning against a post, crying. When he saw me, he stopped and tried to hide what he had been doing, but I already knew something was wrong and asked him what it was.

"I almost lost your Mom last night," he said. He explained that she had experienced a severe allergic reaction in the middle of the night and could barely breathe. Dad had rushed her into town, awakened the family doctor, and driven as quickly as he could to the hospital emergency room. The doctor rode in the hack seat with my mom—scalpel in hand, ready to do a tracheotomy if my mother's throat tightened any more.

My Dad's tears, shameful as they were to him, gave me a warm feeling toward him. They showed me his deep feelings for my mother and the depth of the trauma he had just been through. His tears showed me that deep feelings were a part of life.

The sad side of my father's story is that he probably never shared those feelings with another man. The strong men of our farming community stored their feelings deep inside. They were rarely willing to acknowledge or share them. Deep feelings were expressed only during moments of extreme crisis, when sufficient stress defeated the usual coping mechanisms.

When men have the opportunity to develop deep covenant relationships, they no longer have to hide their feelings. The ability to share their deep, heart-rending emotions help men heal from the woundedness within. As painful as their parting was, Jonathan and David were free to share the depth of their feeling for one another. That final sharing comforted them in the days ahead.

Covenant Friends Share a Lifelong Commitment to One Another

The days ahead were not easy for Jonathan and David. David continued to hide from Saul, and Jonathan continued to fight the Philistines. Eventually Jonathan and Saul were killed in battle on the same day. David mourned their deaths. In time, David became king of Israel and Judah. Despite all that had happened during those years, David never forgot his commitment to Jonathan: "We have sworn friendship with each other in the name of the Lord, saying, 'The Lord is witness between you and me, and between your descendants and my descendants forever'" (1 Samuel 20:42).

This was a powerful commitment for Jonathan and David to make. What man does not worry about his family's future? A man cannot simply assume that his friends will take care of his family, especially when one man has been anointed to be the next king of Israel and the other man is the son of the present king. If a man's friends intend to care for his family in the future, this promise must be directly and clearly communicated. David and Jonathan made an absolute commitment to each other for as long as they would live.

After he became king, David kept his promise. His actions were contrary to what one would have expected, because it was not unusual at that time for a king to kill remaining members of an opposing royal family. However, David located Mephibosheth, a crippled man and the only living son of Jonathan, and brought him into his household.

> "Don't be afraid," David said to him, "for I will surely show you kindness for the sake of your father Jonathan. I will restore to you all the land that belonged to your grandfather Saul, and you will always eat at my table." ... So Mephibosheth ate at David's table like one of the king's sons (2 Samuel 9:7 & 11).

Today there is a crisis of masculine commitment. Will a man stay committed to his friends? Will he stay committed to his relationship with God? Will he stay committed to his wife? David and Jonathan exhibit what deep commitment really means. Their commitment lasted beyond the good times and beyond the life of Jonathan. David's faithfulness lasted as long as he lived. We men today can learn from their example.

Covenant Friendship Makes a Difference in a Man's Life

I wish the story of David and Jonathan had a happy ending, but it does not. Scripture does not reveal that David had a close friendship with anyone other than Jonathan. Although David ruled well, his personal life deteriorated after Jonathan's death. He had an affair that resulted in an unwanted pregnancy. To cover up his sin David arranged for the woman's husband to be killed. Then he married her. The child born to them died a short time after birth.

In addition David, who had once revealed to Jonathan his great frustration regarding Saul's injustice, seemed unable to deal with wrongdoing in his own family. One of his sons raped one of his daughters, and David did nothing. Later, David's son Absalom killed Amnon, the brother who raped his sister. He could not live with the unresolved situation. In shame and anger, David rejected Absalom. This led to an irreparable wound between them that ended in rebellion and war within David's kingdom.

I think David's later life would have been very different if he had found another close friend like Jonathan. David lost his way when Jonathan died. He no longer had a deep friend to turn to when he felt afraid or uncertain. There was no longer a person in his life who would risk everything for him and for whom he would do the same. He no longer had anyone who loved him unconditionally, yet would tell him the hard truth and hold him accountable to it. There was no man in his life with whom he could share his grief and his tears. When Jonathan died, David had to carry the burdens of his life alone.

I do not believe that what we men carry in our hearts today is much different from what David carried. David's story shows the healing power of covenant friendships and the impact masculine support can have on a man's life. It also shows what happens when that support is gone.

I think we men today have to ask the questions: Who is my friend? Who in my life can I turn to when I am in trouble? Who can I trust enough to share the deepest secrets and most painful hurts of my heart? Who will stand beside me and say, "I'll do whatever you need me to do for you?" Who will help me become the man God intended me to be?

A Closer Look

Covenant Friendship—The covenant that two men make in this kind of friendship is an agreement bound by the strength of their individual character and commitment to one another. It is when men give their word to support, defend, aid, and care for one another—whatever the future brings.

Safety or *Safe Place*—The sense of safety that I speak of has several layers of meaning. Safety is physical, emotional, social, intellectual, and spiritual. A son feels safe when he feels secure, protected, provided for, listened to, unconditionally accepted, and valued for who he is. No genuine father-son connection or true friendship can exist without safety. A father demonstrates safety for his son through his physical protection, gentle presence, and fatherly embrace or comfort. He offers safety in his provision of basic material needs. He provides safety through his emotional stability and sensitivity to his son's feelings. He extends safety when he allows his son to be himself. He displays safety when he respects his sons ideas and opinions. He creates safety through his love, acceptance, listening, and honesty. He models ultimate safety through his faith in God. When a son feels safe, he can take risks, pursue his full potential, and stand securely in the world.

Friends also create safety within their relationship. David and Jonathan had a safe relationship. Even in grave danger, David felt secure enough to trust his life to Jonathan. And Jonathan cared enough to risk his life for David. Both knew that God was their ultimate safety net.

For many men, this safety was not experienced in the home or in the father-son relationship. Therefore our churches, support groups, and supportive relationships must be safe places. In Appendix B, *Suggestions for Group Study and Support,* note the *Guidelines for Sharing.* Observance of these guidelines is one way that we can ensure safety in our small group meetings. The guidelines will promote safety in the church and in personal relationships as well.

Sobriety—We experience sobriety when we put aside whatever substance, activity, or person we have used to fill the emptiness or numb the pain. In recovery, we discover that we need our pain. It is our greatest guide. We need sobriety from addictions, codependency, and other numbing behaviors so that we can feel the pain that is hidden in our hearts. Unless we feel our pain, we cannot identify or heal from the wounds that have hindered our growth. Sobriety is an essential element of recovery.

Personal Reflection

1. Who is your closest friend? Who can you turn to when in trouble? Who will stand beside you and say, "I'll do whatever you need me to do for you?" How can you be sure of this friendship?

2. With whom do you feel safe? Who can you trust enough to share the deepest secrets and most painful hurts of your heart? Have you had a safe relationship in the past?

3. Who will help you become the man God intended you to be? What friend of yours will confront you and hold you accountable—with love not shame?

4. Do you believe you have the inner strength necessary to take risks and act courageously to help a friend? What do you lack? Or how have you shown this strength in the past?

5. The Bible says that all good gifts come from above. A friend is a gift, indeed. Ask your heavenly Father for the gift of a good friend. Thank him for the friends you have now. And ask God to make you a faithful and committed friend to those already in your life.

NOTES:

CHAPTER 12

A Vision for the Church as a Healing Community

I believe that the spiritual, emotional, and relational strength of men is the most significant untapped resource in the Christian community today. Although men assume the majority of leadership roles, such as deacon, elder, or board member, women carry on the bulk of relational church ministries. Women are generally more involved than men in Bible studies, prayer ministries, service ministries, and teaching ministries. They also usually lead the way in spiritual teaching within the home and make more of an effort to deepen relationships and communication between family members.

This indicates the crisis of male involvement in the church and home. Our society today has come face to face with the consequences of the father's weak or nonexistent spiritual and emotional presence in the family. The church also faces a crisis. It generally lacks men who are able to minister from the heart. It lacks men who can relate to others not only on an intellectual level but on spiritual and emotional levels as well.

Imagine, if you will, what the church would be like if it were filled with men who had the same kind of commitment to one another that Jonathan and David had. Imagine how the church would be able to care for its members and the downtrodden of society if its men were able to feel deeply, to share their feelings of pain, and to freely express their compassion. Imagine how committed young men would be to God, to their wives, to their children, and to the church if they were guided into manhood under the wise counsel of committed older men, like Eli and Samuel. If Christians today are to fulfill this vision, we must discover what it will take to unleash the power and strength of the masculine soul within the church.

Healing the Hearts of Men

I am convinced that the key to unleashing this great masculine power, strength, and feeling lies in the healing of the father-son wound. This great wound in the hearts of men blocks out deep feelings, prevents spiritually empowered living, and limits masculine growth. Through the process of healing from this deep wound, men become energized and activated. They are set free from spiritual and emotional passivity and begin to live lives of meaning and action.

Healing that enables a man to be spiritually and emotionally empowered requires the active involvement of other men. A man needs a community of men around him who will support and encourage him in his masculine development from birth until death. I believe the community of Christian men today—the church—needs to be doing this.

For a number of years, I have been involved in my own recovery program. I attend twelve-step meetings and have sought out deep relationships with a number of men. Some of these men are mentors, some are close friends, and some look to me as a mentor. I have made progress in dealing with the father-son wound in my life. Still, some of the deep spiritual healing that has needed to take place has come only through the Christian community. Let me share an example of what I mean.

One of the big issues I have to deal with is shame The lack of direct expressions of love and care from my father and most of the other men in my family left me with feelings that I was never quite good enough to receive the affirmation for which I hungered. The church I grew up in focused on outward behavior as the standard for acceptance. Since I could not live within the confines of its prescribed behavior and be a "good boy," I felt shamed by the church too.

The truth is, the men in my life had not experienced anything different themselves, so they did not know how to pass on feelings of affirmation and support. However, these strong messages of shame convinced me that there was more bad in me than good.

During these years I carried that load of shame alone, never imagining that I could share those feelings with anyone especially God who seemed cold and distant to me.

When I began attending First Evangelical Free Church of Fullerton, some of those old messages of shame started to crumble, releasing deep feelings within me. Many times the words of my pastor, Chuck Swindoll, touched my heart and tears would well up. Sometimes, just by listening to the music during worship my tears began to flow. At times I shed tears of sorrow, at other times tears of happiness. At first these powerful feelings embarrassed me, and I tried to hold them back. I just could not imagine a six-foot-five-inch man crying in church.

Then it occurred to me that perhaps the Holy Spirit was awakening me to an area of my feeling life that needed healing. If that were the case, then I was hindering his work by staying in shame and hiding my tears. So I decided that if tears came while I was in church, then I needed to let them come.

After I made this decision it became easier for me to hear and feel what pastor Chuck was sharing. I became more in tune with the deep laughter that came from the depth of his being. I was able to clearly hear the pain or the strong anger in his voice when he spoke about the evils of sin and the destruction it brought into people's lives. As my heart became more open to his messages, my image of God began to change.

You see, my father-son wound and earlier experiences had so distorted my image of God that I could only imagine God the Father to be a God of judgment, a conveyor of shame. If I did not do just the right things to please him, or dared to expose to him what was really in my heart, I was sure God would not want me around. To me God was a judge, not a God who felt sadness, compassion, love ,or pain. When I saw the life and energy that flowed through pastor Chuck as he shared what Scripture revealed about the realities of life, my relationship with God the Father began to change. Looking back, I now realize that God used Chuck Swindoll to touch my heart.

This is just one example of how the Christian community can help bring healing to the hearts of men. Men today bear a countless variety of wounds in their hearts. To heal from their wounds and develop their full potential as men of God it takes strong relationships with father figures of all types. It takes the company of men within the Christian community. And it takes fellowship with God the Father, God the Son, and God the Holy Spirit. This, of course, cannot happen without the strength and power of God's saving grace. But men cannot heal from the deep wounds in their hearts and develop their full, God-given potential without actively facing these issues. Men cannot do this alone, nor can their parents help them do it without the help of others. Every man, from birth until death, needs the support of a community of men who will enable his healing and nurture his full development through the stages of life.

A New Model for Discipleship

If the church is to activate the spiritual strength of its men, we need to expand our concept of discipleship. Traditionally, discipleship has meant training in the disciplines of Bible study, scripture memorization, prayer, and meditation on God's Word and instruction in the basic doctrines of the faith. Today, discipleship needs to be this and much more.

Discipleship must take place on a feeling level as well as on a thinking level. Some men cannot give in both these areas. A disciple who has not dealt with his own father-son wound, who is not connected with his feeling life, may be able to teach Bible study principles, but may not be fully equipped to help a man deal with his daily life and feelings in light of scripture. Since there are no perfect "disciplers," every man needs several—each with his unique blend of strengths—to encourage him toward spiritual and emotional maturity.

We also need to change our idea of who can disciple. Even though we believe that everyone needs to be disciples, the expectations we have of those who disciple is shaming. Most of us are afraid to even attempt to disciple because we believe we almost have to be God in order to meet the expectations. We expect disciples to be able to open a Bible to the right verse instantly, to be able to explain all the cultural and linguistic nuances of every Hebrew or Greek word, to be able to recite the theological and doctrinal implications related to the verse, and to apply all of this perfectly in daily life.

We fail to realize that part of discipleship simply means one man asking another man how he is doing, receiving an honest response, and responding to that need from the depths of his heart and soul. It means that when a man's company is laying off people and he is scared he will lose his job, another man will sit with him and listen to his fears. Perhaps the man who listens will be able to share what God showed him during a similar crisis in his life, put his arm around him and ask what he can do to help or pray with him. When men have this kind of committed, supportive relationship with each other, spiritual growth naturally happens. This is discipleship in real life.

Real discipleship provides a path that moves a boy into deep, holy masculinity. In its most basic form, this kind of discipleship begins at birth. It means that older men, whatever their ages, care enough to invest themselves in the spiritual, emotional, and physical lives of younger men. It means that older men will surround a boy as he becomes a man so that they can help guide and strengthen him through the stages of life. It means they honor and celebrate his deepening status as a man of God.

A man needs to be a disciple spiritually and emotionally in order to discover his feeling life and to be healed from his father-son wound. This discovery usually does not happen on its own. Most men live without feeling much of anything until they reach mid-life and cannot keep their emotions inside any longer. Left on their own, they will do almost anything to keep their feelings at bay. They may go out and get a new car, a new wife, or a new job. They will try everything to avoid dealing with what is in their hearts.

Men need emotional as well as spiritual discipleship. If they lack this kind of nurturing, they will not be able to follow through in their lives and take action. This is why so many seminars and books on Christian marriage and parenting are wasted on men. Men absorb the information, but their hearts are not touched because they are so disconnected from their emotions. A man may read that he should spend more time with his kids, but unless he has felt the pain of his own father's absence, he does not really understand what his absence means to his children. A man may be told that he should do something special for his wife's birthday, so he may buy her candy and take her out to dinner. She may feel special for the moment, but she really wants her husband to respond to her inner feelings, to understand her world. When a husband begins to connect with his wife on a feeling level, he is able to give of himself in ways his wife really needs.

Spiritual and emotional discipleship touches the hearts of men. Until the hearts of men and women are touched, the ministry of the church is limited. When men connect with their feelings and begin to heal their father-son wound, they can have a powerful ministry. Let me tell you about Jim, a sixty-five-year-old man who got in touch with his feelings of woundedness and completely changed his life and ministry.

When Jim heard me speak about the father-son wound, he realized some important things about himself. Years ago he had gone to work in his dad's company to gain his approval. Long after his father had died, he had continued to keep the company going even though this was not what he really wanted to do with his life. When he discovered this inner motivation, he sold the company and retired. Then he began building bridges to his adult children, letting them know he was sorry that he had not been available to them when they were younger. Now he spends one day a week volunteering at the church, and he teaches a Sunday school class for 4 year old children because he realizes that little kids need older men to be active in their lives. He is always looking for opportunities to do things with his grandchildren. He also spends time each week distributing food to the poor.

This man has so much to give, and he is giving it! No one has to tell him he ought to be doing what he is doing. It just naturally flows from him. He was able to connect with his father-son wound, acknowledge his failures, and live a completely new, spiritually activated life. There is an awesome power at work when a man's heart is healed and he truly becomes spiritually alive.

Initiating a Man through the Stages of Life

My hope for Christian men today is that they will become emotionally and spiritually activated so they can take steps toward nurturing and disciplining one another in all aspects of masculine growth. I envision a whole community of men being available to initiate and support one another through all stages of life. I hope that a boy's life will be touched by men of all generations—older men, middle-aged men, and men in their early twenties. I hope for men who will show concern for him, talk with him, teach him, and pray with him. Men of all ages need this kind of nurturing throughout life. I would like to share with you some examples of how this can be done.

When a young man graduates from high school, the men of the church could rally around him. They could acknowledge his entrance into a new stage of life and renew their commitment to be there for him as he gets older. Perhaps they could spend an evening with the young man and share some of the things they went through at that time of life. They could share some of their fears, expectations, and some of the ways they failed. By sharing their feelings and experiences, the older men could show the young man that it is not shameful to be afraid and that it is okay to fail. They could show him that they are available to help him make it through the difficult times and to celebrate the good times.

Another opportunity to initiate a young man occurs when he gets a bit older and becomes serious about dating. During this crucial period the older men could take the young man away and talk with him about relationships with women and marriage. A young man needs the perspective of older men at this time in life. Most young men imagine a woman to be an all-loving, all-caring, all-sexual, all-nurturing, magical person. A young man needs to learn that no woman on earth will ever match up to what he thinks a woman is. He needs older men to bring some reality into his expectations.

Then, when a man is ready to get married, he needs the insight and wisdom older men can offer. A man needs, from the beginning, a long-term view of marriage. It is important for him to understand that marriage is different in your twenties, forties, and sixties. He needs to know that a twenty-year-old's image of marriage will not last for a lifetime because each person has different issues to work through and each will change. He must realize that marriage is the foundation through which those issues are resolved and through which those changes occur. He needs to know that in marriage there are times of closeness and passion as well as times of coldness. He needs reassurance that when the passion dies down, it is no big deal. It just means that he and his wife have something to work on in the relationship when passion runs low, it is not time to hire a divorce attorney. It is time to work on what is happening inside so that things will be okay again. Men who have been married for thirty or fifty years, as well as men who have been through a divorce, have something valuable to share with younger men.

When a man learns that he is to become a father, fathers of all generations need to gather around him, celebrate with him and disciple him in his new role. A man needs to adjust his expectations of his wife when children enter the family. He needs to understand that he will not always be first anymore. Men do not like that! Unless other men prepare him for these changes, a new father can become angry and jealous and behave like a little boy.

As a man's children grow up, he continues to require the guidance of other men. He needs to understand how his role in life will change as he matures. He will profit from the perspective of men who changed their attitudes toward work in order to have more time with their children, and he will learn from the hindsight of those who did not change. He needs to hear the pain in the heart of the father of a teenager who cannot talk to his son anymore because of the damage to their relationship. He will require an ongoing commitment of support and encouragement from other fathers.

When a man becomes a grandfather, he needs the guidance and support of other men as he assumes his new role. Other grandfathers can help him to learn how to be a grandfather, perhaps how to connect with grandchildren who live far away. Other grandfathers can help him understand what it means to be the husband of a grandmother. A new grandfather needs to hear the stories of younger men who had close relationships with their grandfather—to hear them talk about the memorable times they spent with them

Men need these kinds of initiatory experiences throughout life. These experiences should not be limited to the milestones of a man's family life. They need to include the turning points of his career and other interests as well. Prime times for initiatory experiences include a man's graduation from college, his completion of advanced degrees, his promotions in corporate or military service, changes in his career, and his retirement. Initiation ceremonies can also recognize the milestones of a man's creative and personal development, such as the publication of his writings, his placement in an athletic contest, the acceptance of his work in an art exhibition or a host of other personal accomplishments.

A Lifetime of Support for Men in Need

Initiation provides the foundation through which a man receives ongoing support from the male Christian community. The initiation process awakens a man to the fact that other men can be a resource for him throughout life. It helps him realize that other men will be there for him as he works through his feelings, handles new situations and makes difficult decisions.

Men need this kind of support. Several years ago I was betrayed by a friend and business associate. This betrayal caused a great deal of pain and harm to me and others. My friend's actions produced one of the greatest wounds in my life and jeopardized a lifetime of work and diligence on my part. At the time I plunged into depression, fear, shame, and worry. I doubted my ability to continue my work and seriously considered selling everything I owned, taking my wife and children to a remote part of the country, and finding some other way to support my family.

As you can imagine, I am not fun to be around when I am in that state of mind. I live on the verge of making bad decisions that could affect the rest of my life. I am tense and cannot sleep. Sadly, the people I love feel the impact of the turmoil within me. During times like these my only solution is to turn to God and to other men. Just as David needed Jonathan, I need men who are deeply committed to me and will stand by me. I need men who will help me work through my fear and worry and help me grow into a different spiritual, emotional, and physical state.

I was fortunate to have had two friends who stayed close beside me throughout that horrible time. These men had every reason to abandon me, for my depression was deep and my feelings of shame were strong. Still, they stuck with me through the trouble. They affirmed me, encouraged me, and strengthened me. They helped to set realistic boundaries with the friend who had betrayed me. They helped me identify the limits of my responsibility and enabled me to see how I had overlooked my friend's dark side. As these two friends walked with me, the bond between us grew stronger, and God's ministry of grace became more real to me.

All men need relationships with other men who have what it takes to keep their commitments to each other during difficult times—men who are not afraid to be truthful and real. Many men carry deep, deep hurts that need to be healed. Sometimes a man begins to remember the sexual or emotional abuse he received as a young boy and feels as if he is losing control of his anger and fear. Sometimes a man loses his job and is so overwhelmed with shame from his past that he cannot bring himself to get out of bed in the morning and look for work. Sometimes a man reaches a crisis in mid-life when he feels as if time is running short so he plunges into a destructive whirlwind of adolescent-type activity.

In all of these situations and more, men need to be ministered to by other men. They need the support of men who will offer comfort in their pain and encouragement as they struggle toward healing. Ministering to another man may mean holding and comforting him when he has flashbacks of sexual abuse. It may mean gently listening to a man who for decades has never revealed the fearsome details of his darkest combat days in battle. It may mean affirming a man who is apprehensive about making a career change. It may mean sharing tears with the man who helplessly watched his best buddy die following a mortar attack.

This is what I believe men's ministry is all about. Men are naturally afraid that other men will reject them if they share their deepest feelings and most intense struggles. So they keep their emotions to themselves for a long time. It takes a greatly hardened heart and/or tremendous amounts of alcohol, drugs, food, work, or sex to keep these feelings locked inside. The ongoing ministry of a community of Christian men can help men heal from the wounds in their heart—old wounds as well as new. It can help them grow more fully into Christian manhood can help them put into action what Christ planted in their hearts when they became Christians.

My Hope for the Church

This is an exciting time to live within the Christian community. During the past several years a movement has begun within the church. We have been changing how we view ourselves, how we relate to Scripture, and how we go about life and ministry. Our fundamental belief that Jesus Christ is the Son of God, our Lord and Savior, remains unshakable. It is a great comfort to have the sound principles of scripture to guide us in an ever-changing and increasingly confusing world. It has also become apparent that God would have his people open their hearts to his loving touch and to one another.

The last words of the Old Testament speak of healed hearts:

> See, I will send you the prophet Elijah before that great and dreadful day of the LORD comes. He will turn the hearts of the fathers to their children, and the hearts of the children to their fathers... (Malachi 4:5-6).

The crises we face in the family, the church, and society make it apparent that the hearts of fathers must he restored to their children and that the hearts of children must be restored to their fathers. For several reasons, I believe the Christian community is the place for this to happen.

First, the Christian community is one of the few communities left in our society. At one time people were born, lived and died in the same towns or neighborhoods. Today that rarely happens. Even today's families do not provide the sense of community they once did. Present divorce rates mean that many children grow up with several sets of grandparents, parents, and siblings. The church is the one community that can provide people with an identity, and a place to learn and grow from birth until death.

Second, the church provides a common standard of values and beliefs that are based on the authority of Scripture. Although a common standard of values existed in our culture fifty years ago, there is no longer a culturally accepted moral authority. Fifty years ago most people—Christian or not—would agree that it was wrong to have an extramarital affair. Today many people do not even recognize the need for or legitimacy of moral authority. As society continues to disintegrate, the church is the only community of people who are willing to live life according to the unchanging principles of scripture.

Third, God has always viewed His people as a community and as a family. The earthly father's role is important, but no father can be everything for his son. A son needs an incredible number of "fathers" in his life. This is where the men of the Christian community can step in and make a tremendous difference.

When men start allowing God to touch their hearts, and when they start reaching out to touch the hearts of other men, they will make a tremendous difference in the church and in the community as well. When men become actively involved in touching the hearts and lives of other men, they start helping one another, listening to one another, and praying with one another. They begin to look forward to spending time together and start taking an active role in the church. Men who are spiritually activated take the living gospel into their communities. They reach out to the homeless and feed the hungry. They repair the widow's leaky roof. They become involved in the lives of boys who do not have a strong connection with their fathers. When men become spiritually activated, men's ministry means much more than golf tournaments and steak frys. Spiritually activated men are empowered to minister to others from the depths of their hearts.

A new pastor came to a church that had become close-minded and had lost its zeal for winning souls. He convinced them that God wanted them to begin an active outreach to the community around them, starting with the junior college across the street. Some people resisted the idea. After all, the college students would not have much money to donate to church projects and might not dress as well as the long-standing church members. After much prayer, the pastor prevailed and the outreach began.

Not long afterward the church was once again filled to overflowing every Sunday. Some of those who resisted the outreach still grumbled, but most of the congregation supported it wholeheartedly. One Sunday, however, the congregation's commitment was put to the test.

The service had already begun when a young man walked right down the center aisle and sat down cross-legged right in the aisle!

He had obviously had a rough night. His hair and clothes were messed up and he smelled. The pastor could hear the mumbling and felt as if his entire ministry was on the line. Just as he was about to say something to the young man, an old man stood up and, with the aid of his cane, began slowly walking down the aisle toward the young man. The pastor recognized him at once as one of the charter members who gave generously to the church. As usual, this old gentleman was dressed in his best suit The pastor's heart trembled. He held his breath and waited to see what would happen next.

The old man had made his way down the aisle. He stood next to the young man, leaned on his cane, and slowly lowered himself to sit next to him. Together, the young man and old man sat cross-legged, waiting to hear the pastor's message. To a hushed crowd the pastor said, "The sermon I have to preach doesn't compare to the message God has just given us."[1]

A Closer Look

Christian Community—When I refer to the Christian community, I mean the fellowship of people united together in worship, service, and mutual encouragement because of their common faith in Jesus Christ. This can be the local church, the support group that meets in a home, two or three Christian friends gathered for coffee or a meal, or the Church around the world. Wherever Christians fellowship and come together, the Christian community exists.

Discipleship—The kind of Christian discipleship that I envision among men includes all the traditional components of discipleship plus the added initiation process of masculine development. Discipleship should be a life long process for all members of the male Christian community. Every stage of a man's life requires the support and encouragement of other men. A man should never end his commitment to his own emotional and spiritual development. And he should always look for ways to give his life away to other men.

Prayer—Prayer is communication and fellowship with God. It is most effective when it is honest and frequent. It is fitting to complain to God, to lament before God, to thank God, to share the details of our lives with God, to praise God, and to talk to God as we would talk to a trusted friend. Avoid "wish-list" prayers that ask God for something. Our best pursuit in prayer is to seek God's will for us, and to seek the power to carry out God's will.

Personal Reflection

1. What has been your experience with the Christian community and in particular the community of Christian men?

2. In what ways have you experienced affirmation or support from the Christian community? In what ways have you experienced shame or rejection? How have these experiences affected you?

3. What is your current concept of discipleship? What do you need from your Christian community to help you reshape your life toward godly masculine development?

4. Do you have a committed group of Christian men with whom to share your life? Who are the Christian men in your life that you look up to? What is it that you see and admire about them?

5. Take a few moments to reflect on the lessons you have learned through this book. Ask God to continue to give you understanding about the issues important to your heart. Thank God for his perfect fatherhood and for his perfect love for you.

NOTES:

Appendix "A"

A Word about Brain Chemistry

Counseling and psychotherapy—even re-parenting, mentoring, and spirituality with 12-step recovery—cannot address every need. The immaturity and childishness we see in adults may actually be a problem in brain chemistry—not bad character. Impulsive behavior, hyperactivity, and fits of rage may be medical and not moral issues. And all the counseling in the world will not correct some forms of depression and moodiness.

Thanks to advancements in medicine, a certain kind of brain-imaging known as a SPECT scan can pinpoint over or underactive, or damaged, areas of the brain. Doctors can use this information to prescribe medication and balance a patient's brain chemistry. This often allows the patient to experience immediate relief from life-controlling problems. Even young men with lifelong conduct disorders can experience behavior change.

An imbalance in brain chemistry or a problem in the physiology of the brain can cause a person to pursue behaviors, chemicals, and relationships to soothe moods, stimulate concentration, and feel normal. Risk-taking or daredevil behaviors can provide a large dose of adrenaline and calm the hyperactive or focus the scattered. Waking up to the "worry of the day" can provide that same fix of natural speed that allows the disorganized brain to bring order to life. But there is a cost. Risk-taking and daredevil activity can lead to injury or death. And chronic worry can lead to an ever-present sense of doom and a constant state of alert. Tense shoulders, headaches, irritated bowels, autoimmune diseases like fibromyalgia, and chronic-fatigue can all result.

Sugar, high carbohydrate foods, and alcohol all bring a chemical change and soothing effect to the limbic system in the brain. This will also affect the reward pathways in our brain and allow us to feel good about ourselves. The person who has a problem in this area of the brain might receive compliments all day, but the good words just bounce off. They hear the compliments, but just can't accept them. But after a few drinks, a few bags of M&Ms, or a few peanut-butter and jelly sandwiches, the person can feel good about him or herself. The risk, however, is obesity, alcoholism, depression, and a host of other health and social ills.

People pleasing, caretaking, and other codependent relationships can be mood-altering experiences that trigger changes in a person's brain. The fact that we feel better when we control or enmesh ourselves in the lives of others can be a result of brain chemistry. In the end, the codependent relationship will not lead to lasting or positive changes.

If a person's problems are related to imbalance in brain chemistry or inactivity in brain function, there are specific medical interventions that can be help. For example, if you constantly get "stuck" on certain thoughts, you may have a problem with your cingulate system. If you have trouble focusing your attention you may need a prefrontal cortex prescription. If you're plagued by anxiety, the problem may lie in your basal ganglia system. If you find it hard to connect meaningfully with others, you may need to correct a faulty deep limbic system. If you can't tame your temper, your temporal lobes may be to blame. It is important to take responsibility if problems—that you have worked on in therapy or with medications—continue to persist. You may need a more accurate diagnosis with SPECT Brain Imaging. For a more detailed discussion of these problems and their treatment see the book *Change Your Brain, Change Your Life* by neuropsychiatrist Daniel Amen, M.D.

f

Also see Dr. Amen's website:
http://www.amenclinic.com.

Appendix "B"

Suggestions for Small Group Study and Support

I believe that everyone, who seeks healing from the brokenness and pain of a less-than-perfect father-son connection, needs the support of others. For that reason, I offer some suggestions for small group study and support. The following are common questions and concerns about the organization and make-up of a small group that is formed for the purpose of study and support.

Who should participate in group?
Anyone who relates to the topics and needs discussed in this book should participate. No one should attend as an observer. No one should attend for another person. No one should attend to provide input to the group.

Is a mixed group of men and women appropriate?
No support or study group for the male issues should be mixed. Separate groups should be formed for other issues and topics.

Where should we meet?
Many churches and community groups will provide space for support groups. A private home is a good place as well.

Who should lead the group?
Like twelve-step groups, the best form of leadership is the "group conscience." Decisions should be made by the group as a whole. Even questions of leadership and logistics should be considered together—no one left out. If a church or community organization is sponsoring the group, then existing leadership from within the church or organization would be appropriate. Still, the wise leader will take input and suggestions from the members of the study or support group.

After an introductory meeting(s) should the group be closed to newcomers and consist of only those willing to make a commitment to the group?
This is a decision left best to the group as a whole. There are good reasons to close a group and good reasons to keep a group open. A closed group

provides extra safety for some. An open group provides greater access and openness to those in need outside the group.

What should be the meeting format?
Any format that is agreed upon by group is fine. I have offered a suggested group format later in Appendix B. A fixed routine, whatever the format, provides safety, structure, and stability week after week. There should be enough flexibility to allow the personality and special needs of the group to be expressed.

How long should the group meet?
This is a decision for the whole group. But the possibilities are broad. A group might form to go through the book rather quickly. After an initial meeting, a group could discuss one chapter a week. In this case, the members would have to read the material in advance of the meeting. Or a group might choose to proceed at a more leisurely pace. The group might read and discuss the material in the meeting, taking one section at a time. If the meeting is intended primarily for support, rather than study, the book would be used differently. A portion of the book might be read as a topic for discussion—without concern for a thorough reading or study of the text. This kind of a support group could meet indefinitely or for an agreed upon length of time.

What about a phone list? Should we share personal phone numbers with other group members and call one another for support outside the meeting?
Many twelve-step groups provide a phone list for mutual support during the week. Support from one another is always a good idea, but the decision to release personal phone numbers should always left up to each individual.

Guidelines for Sharing

A small group that has come together to support one another must be a safe place. The following guidelines for sharing can ensure that safety—if they are followed. It is important to refer to these guidelines before every meeting and to discuss them in depth at the first meeting. I've provided questions to spur group discussion and personal reflection on the guidelines.

❑ Keep comments brief, take turns talking, and don't interrupt others.

❑ Speak personally: I, me, my—not you, we, they.

❑ Be honest, sharing both successes and struggles.

❑ Don't fix, advise, or rescue others—respect each person's right to self-expression without comment.

❑ Take responsibility—don't blame or judge others.

❑ Avoid cross talk—speak to the entire group.

❑ Keep confidence to ensure an atmosphere of safety and openness.

❑ Respect the needs of others by asking permission to express concern with a hug or a touch—many are uncomfortable with physical contact.

❑ Avoid gossip—share your own needs and refrain from talking about a person who is absent.

❑ Hold others accountable for their behavior only if they ask you to do so.

Personal Reflection

1. Which of the *Guidelines for Sharing* is most important to you? Why?

2. What do you need most from others to feel safe in a support group meeting?

3. What is your past experience with support groups? Share both your good and not-so-good experiences.

4. What do you hope to receive from this support group?

5. What do you believe you have to offer other members in the group?

Suggested Meeting Format

The following is a suggest meeting format for a small group that is formed to study this book and support one another through the process.

Opening Prayer

Any prayer that acknowledges God is appropriate. A prayer that is commonly used in twelve-steps meeting is the short version of Serenity Prayer by Reinhold Niebuhr:

> *God, grant me the serenity to accept the things I cannot change, the courage to change the things I can, and the wisdom to know the difference.*

Higher Focus

Someone from the group should come prepared to share a five minute (no more) inspirational or spiritual reading. It can be a poem, a meditation from a published source, a passage of scripture, or a short story. The important thing is to lift everyone's focus to a higher, more positive place. As the Apostle Paul said, "*Whatever is true, whatever is noble, whatever is right, whatever is pure, whatever is lovely, whatever is admirable—if anything is excellent or praiseworthy—think about such things.*"

Introduction and Personal Sharing—Highs and Lows

Go around the group and allow each man present to introduce himself (first names only) and share the high point and the low point of his previous week. Everyone should know he is free to "pass" and refrain from sharing without explanation. We share high and low points to stay in touch at a feeling level. Rather than report events or offer opinions, it is better to share feelings. When we share a high and a low, we broaden and balance our emotional connection with others.

Topic for Sharing

An agreed upon portion of the book should be read. The group may take turns reading one paragraph at time or a volunteer may read the entire portion. Everyone should know that he is free to "pass" and refrain from reading out loud.

After the reading, allow each participant to share his personal experience or feelings related to the material covered. The *A Closer Look* and *Personal Reflection* at the end of each chapter can help focus sharing. When everyone who desires to share has done so, another portion may be read as time allows.

Concluding Comments and Requests for Support
Before the meeting dismisses, everyone should have the opportunity to share one final and brief comment or make a request for support or prayer. The final comment may be an insight that was gained from the meeting. It might be a word of thanks or an affirmation. It might be a final thought related to the topic. Requests for support or prayer should be directed to the entire group. No immediate, individual response or feedback should be offered. And no group prayer should be offered for the request unless the person has asked for immediate group prayer.

Concluding Prayer
Any agreed upon prayer is appropriate. Many support groups form a circle, hold hands, and conclude with the *Lord's Prayer*:

Our Father, Who art in heaven, hallowed be thy name. Thy kingdom come. Thy will be done, on earth as it is in heaven. Give us this day our daily bread. And forgive us our trespasses, as we forgive those who trespass against us. And lead us not into temptation, but deliver us from evil. For thine is the kingdom and the power and the glory, forever and ever. Amen.

Appendix "C"

Recovery Resources

§

ADD Anonymous
Website: http://www.members.aol.com/addanon/

Alcoholics Anonymous (AA)
475 Riverside Dr., New York, NY 10015
Phone: 212-870-3400; Fax: 212-870-3003
Website: http://www.alcoholics-anonymous.org

Adult Children of Alcoholics (ACA or AcoA)
PO Box 3216, Torrance, CA 90510
Phone: 310-534-1815;
E-mail: info@adultchildren.org
Website: http://adultchildren.org

Al-Anon/Alateen Family Groups Headquarters, Inc.
1600 Corporate Landing Parkway, Virginia Beach, VA 23454-5617
Phone: 757-563-1600, 888-4Al-anon (888-425-2666); Fax: 757-563-1655
E-mail: wso@al-anon.org
Website: http://al-anon.alateen.org

Clutterers Anonymous (CLA)
PO Box 25884, Santa Ana, CA 92799-5884
Website: http://clutterers-anonymous.org/

Co-Dependents Anonymous (CoDA)
105 E. Grant Road, Tucson, AZ 85705
Phone: 520-882-5705
Website: http://mpoweru.com/alano/co-depen.htm
Website: http://coda-tvcc.org/

Co-Anon Family Groups World Services, Inc
PO Box 12124, Tucson, AZ 85732-2124

Phone: 770-928-5122 Atlanta, GA; 714-647-6698 Orange County, CA;
818-377-4317 Los Angeles, CA; 520-513-5028 Tucson, AZ
Website: http://co-anon.org

Cocaine Anonymous (C.A.), Inc.
3740 Overland Ave., # C, Los Angeles, CA 90034
Phone: 310-559-5833; Fax: 310-559-2554
National Referral Line: 800-347-8998
Email: cawso@ca.org; Website: http://ca.org

Debtors Anonymous
PO Box 920888, Needham, MA 02492-0009
Phone: 781-453-2743; Fax: 781-453-2745
E-mail: new@debtorsanonymous.org
Website: http://debtorsanonymous.org

Emotions Anonymous International (EA)
PO Box 4245, St. Paul MN 55104-0245
Phone: 651-647-9712; Fax: 651-647-1593
E-mail: info@emotionsanonymous.org
Website: http://emotionsanonymous.org

Families Anonymous WSO & Info. Services, 800-736-9805

Gamblers Anonymous (GA)
PO Box 17173, Los Angeles, CA 90017
Phone: 213-386-8789, 310-478-212; Fax: 213-386-0030
E-mail: isomain@gamblersanonymous.org
Website: http://gamblersanonymous.org

Marijuana Anonymous (MA)
PO Box 2912, Van Nuys, CA 91404
Phone: 800-766-6779
E-mail: maws98@aol.com; Website: http://marijuana—anonymous.org

Narcotics Anonymous (NA)
PO Box 9999, Van Nuys, CA 91409
19737 Nordhoff Place, Chatsworth, CA 91311
Phone: 818-773-9999; Fax: 818-700-0700
E-mail: info@na.org; Website: http://wsoinc.com

Nicotine Anonymous (NicA)
PO Box 591777, San Francisco, CA 94159-1777
Phone: 415-750-0328
E-mail: info@nicotine-anonymous.org
Website: http://nicotine-anonymous.org/

Overeaters Anonymous (OA)
PO Box 44020, Rio Rancho, NM 87174-4020
6075 Zenith Ct. NE, Rio Rancho, NM 87124
Phone: 505-891-2664; Fax: 505-891-4320
E-mail: overeatr@technet.nm.org
Website: http://www.oa.org

Phobics Anonymous
Website: http://pilot.infi.net/~susanf/12ofphob.htm

Pills Anonymous
Phone: 714-978-9685
www.pillsanonymous.com

Recoveries Anonymous Universal Services
PO Box 1212, East Northport, NY 11731
Website: http://r-a.org

S-Anon International Family Groups (SA)
PO Box 111242, Nashville, TN 37222-1242
Phone: 800-210-8141
E-mail: sanon@sanon.org; Website: http://sanon.org

Sex Addicts Anonymous (SAA)
Website: http://sexaa.org
Phone: 800-477-8191

Sex and Love Addicts Anonymous (SLAA)
1550 NE Loop 410, Ste 118, San Antonio, TX 78209
Phone: 210-828-7922
Website: http://slaafws.org

Sexaholics Anonymous (S.A.)
PO Box 3565, Brentwood, TN 37024
Phone: 615-370-6062; Fax: 615-370-0882
E-mail: ca@sa.org or saico@sa.org; Website: http://sa.org

Sexual Compulsives Anonymous (SCA)
PO Box 1585, Old Chelsea Station, New York, NY 10011
Int'l Info: 212-606-3778; Phone: 800-977-4325, 212-439-1123
E-mail: info@sca—recovery.org; Website: http://sca-recovery.org

Twelve Step Home Page (resources for the online community)
Website: http://twelvestep.com

CHRISTIAN 12 STEP ORGANIZATIONS

Alcoholics for Christ
Website: http://alcoholicsforchrist.com

National Association for Christian Recovery
PO Box 215, Brea, CA 92822-0215
Voicemail: 714-529-6227; Fax: 714-529-1120
E-mail: dryan@christianrecovery.com
Website: http://christianrecovery.com

Overcomers Outreach Inc.
PO Box 922950
Sylmar, CA 91392-2950
Phone: 800-310-3001; Fax: 818-833-1546
E-mail: info@overcomersoutreach.org
Website: http://overcomersoutreach.org

Spirit of Hope (ADD/ADHD Support)
PO Box 53642, Irvine, CA 92619-3642
Phone: 714-308-2494
E-mail: seiden@pacbell.net

Appendix "D"

Suggested Reading

Adams, Kenneth M. Ph.D. *Silently Seduced: When Parents Make Their Children Partners*. Deerfield Beach, FL: Health Communications, Inc., 1991.

Adult Children. *The Secrets of Dysfunctional Families*. Deerfield Beach, FL: Health Communications, Inc., 1988.

Alcoholics Anonymous. *Alcoholics Anonymous, "The Big Book."* New York: Alcoholics Anonymous World Services, Inc.

—. *Twelve Steps—Twelve Traditions*. New York: Alcoholics Anonymous World Services, Inc.

Alsdurf, James and Phyllis. *Battered into Submission*. InterVarsity Press, 1989.

Amen, Daniel, M.D. *Change Your Brain, Change Your Life*. New York: Random House, 1999.

Beattie, Melody. *Codependent No More*. New York: Harper Collins Publishers, 1987.

—. *Beyond Codependency: And Getting Better All the Time*. New York: Walker, 1990.

Bly, Robert. *Iron John*. Addison-Wesley, 1990.

Boteach, Shmuel. *Kosher Sex: a Recipe for Passion and Intimacy*. New York: Main Street, 2000.

Bradshaw, John. *Bradshaw on: The Family—A New Way of Creating Solid Self-esteem*. Deerfield Beach, FL: Health Communications, Inc., 1996.

—. *Family Secrets: What You Don't Know Can Hurt You*. New York : Bantam Books, 1995.

—. *Healing the Shame That Binds You*. Deerfield Beach, FL: Health Communications, 1988.

Carder, Dave; Henslin, Earl; Cloud, Henry; Townsend, John; Brawand, Alice. *Secrets of Your Family Tree: Healing for Adult Children Of Dysfunctional Families*. Moody Press, 1991.

Carnes, Patrick. *Contrary to Love: Helping the Sexual Addict*. Minneapolis, MN: CompCare Publishers, 1989.

—. *Don't Call It Love: Recovery from Sexual Addiction*. New York: Bantam Books, 1991.

—. *A Gentle Path through the Twelve Steps.* Minneapolis, MN: CompCare Publishers, 1993.

—. *Sexual Anorexia: Overcoming Sexual Self-Hatred.* Center City, MN: Hazelden, 1997.

Cosby, Bill. *Fatherhood.* Dolphin Doubleday, 1986.

Coopersmith, Stanley. *The Antecedents of Self-esteem.* San Francisco: W.H. Freeman, 1967.

Dalbey, Gordon. *Father and Son: The Wound, The Healing, The Call to Manhood.* Thomas Nelson Publishers, 1992.

—. *Healing the Masculine Soul.* Word Publishing, 1988.

De Becker, Gavin. *The Gift of Fear: Survival Signals that Protect Us from Violence.* Boston: Little, Brown, 1997.

Fisher, Robert. *The Knight in the Rusty Armor.* Wilshire Book Company, 1987.

Friends in Recovery. *The 12 Steps—A Spiritual Journey.* San Diego: RPI Publishing, Inc., 1994.

— with Jerry S. *Meditations for the Twelve Steps—A Spiritual Journey.* San Diego: RPI Publishing, Inc., 1993.

Goulter, Barbara and Minninger, Joan Ph.D. *The Father-daughter Dance.* New York: G.P. Putnam's Sons, 1993.

Hallowell, Edward, M.D. and Ratey, John J., M.D. *Driven to Distraction.* New York: Pantheon Books, 1994.

Halverstadt, Jonathan Scott, M.S. *ADD & Romance: Finding Fulfillment in Love, Sex, & Relationships.* Taylor Publishing Company, 1999.

Henslin, Earl R. Psy.D.(co-author). *Secrets of Your Family Tree.* Moody Press, 1991.

—. *Forgiven and Free: Learn How Bible Heros with Feet of Clay Are Models for Your Recovery.* Nashville: Thomas Nelson, [1994] 1991.

—. *The Cliff's Edge: Heaven Sent Help on a Harley—Hell Came in Other Ways.* Irvine, CA: Spirit of Hope Publishing, 2001.

—. *You Are Your Father's Daughter: The Nurture Every Daughter Needs— The Longing When It's Lost.* Irvine, CA: Spirit of Hope Publishing, 2000.

Hicks, Robert. *Un-Easy Manhood.* Oliver Nelson, 1991.

Hunter, Mic. *Abused Boys.* Lexington Books, 1990.

Keyes, Ralph. *Sons on Fathers.* Harper Collins, 1991

Kritsberg, Wayne. *The Adult Children of Alcoholics Syndrome: from Discovery to Recovery.* Deerfield Beach, FL: Health Communications, Inc., 1986.

Levinson, Daniel. *The Seasons of a Man's Life.* Ballantine Books, 1978.

Liebman, Wayne. *Tending the Fire: The Ritual Men's Group.* Ally Press, 1991.

McClung, Floyd Jr. *The Father Heart of God.* Harvest House Publishers, 1985

Miller, Keith. *A Hunger for Healing*. Harper Collins, 1992.

Millett, Craig Ballard. *In God's Image*. San Diego: LuraMedia, Inc., 1991.

Osherson, Samuel. *Finding Our Fathers*. Ballantine Books, 1986.

Peale, Norman Vincent. *This Incredible Century*. Tyndale House Publishers, 1991.

Penner, Clifford. *Men and Sex: Discovering Greater Love, Passion & Intimacy with Your Wife*. Nashville: Thomas Nelson Publishers, 1997.

Scull, Charles, editor. *Fathers & Sons and Daughters: Exploring Fatherhood, Renewing the Bond*. Los Angeles: J.P. Tarcher, 1992.

Seiden, Jerry. *Divine or Distorted: God As We Understand God*. Irvine, CA: Spirit of Hope Publishing, 1993.

—. *Michael's Stable: The Best Gift Is to Belong*. Irvine, CA: Spirit of Hope Publishing, 1999.

—. *Jabez the Man: Why God's Heart Was Moved*. Irvine, CA: Spirit of Hope Publishing, 2001.

—. *The Heart Set Free: Healing for Wounded Hearts—Freedom from Repeated Mistakes*. Irvine, CA: Spirit of Hope Publishing, 2001.

Sheppard, Kay. *Food Addiction: The Body Knows*. Health Communications, Inc., 1989.

Smith, David. *Men Without Fnends*. Thomas Nelson Publishers, 1990.

Sorenson, Amanda and Stephen, eds. *Time with God: The New Testament for Busy People*. Word Publishing, 1991.

Thompson, Keith, ed. *To Be A Man: In Search of the Deep Masculine*. Jeremy P. Tarcher, Inc., 1991.

Wegscheider-Cruse, Sharon. *Learning To Love Yourself*. Deerfield Beach, FL: Health Communications, Inc., 1987.

Whitfield, Charles. *Healing the Child Within*. Deerfield Beach, FL: Health Communications, Inc., 1987.

Willard, Dallas. *The Divine Conspiracy: Rediscovering Our Hidden Life in God*. San Francisco: HarperSanFrancisco, 1998.

Wilson-Schaef, Anne. *Escape from Intimacy*. Harper and Row, 1989.

Woititz, Janet. *Struggle For Intimacy*. Deerfield Beach, FL: Health Communications, Inc., 1985.

—. *Adult Children of Alcoholics*. Deerfield Beach, FL: Health Communications,

End Notes

Inc., [1983] 1991.

Chapter One:
1. Rader, Dotson; "What Love Means," *Parade* (March 8, 1992) pg. 4.
2. Ibid., pg.4.
3. Watson, Thomas J. Jr. and Petre, Peter; *Father, Son, & Co.* (New York: Bantam Books, 1991) pg. 288.
4. Bly, Robert; "Men's Initiation Rites" *Utne Reader*, (April/May 1986): 45.

Chapter Two:
1. Adams, Kenneth M. *Silently Seduced: When Parents Make Their Children Partners* (Deerfield Beach, Florida: Health Communications, Inc., 1992) pgs. 9-10.

Chapter Three:
1. Patterson, James and Kim, Peter; *The Day America Told the Truth: What People Realty Believe About Everything that Really Matters* (New York, Prentice Hall Press, 1991) pg. 25.
2. Ibid., pgs. 25, 26.
3. Ibid., edited statistics from throughout the book.
4. Covey, Stephen R. *The Seven Habits of Highly Effective People: Powerful Lessons in Personal Change* (New York: Simon & Shuster, 1989) pg. l8.
5. Ibid., pg. 18.
6. *Utne Reader*, April/May 1986. pg. 44. This article written by Gail Early and originally appeared in the *Chico News and Review*, July 11,1985.
7. Ibid., pg. 44.

Chapter Four:
1. Watson, Thomas J. Jr. and Petre, Peter; *Father Son & Co.* (New York: Bantam Books, 1991) pgs. 366, 367.
2. Adapted from a story told by Robert Bly on the audio cassette; *Fairy Tales for Men and Women*, available from Ally Press.

Chapter Five:
1. Watson, Thomas J. Jr. and Petre, Peter; *Father, Son & Co.* (New York: Bantam Books, 1991) pg 288.
2. Osherson, Samuel; *Finding Our Fathers* (New York: Fawcett Columbine, 1986) pgs. 54, 55.

3. From a survey of pastors from the Fuller Institute of Church Growth and reported to the Care Givers Forum in Colorado Springs, Colorado, November, 1991 as reported in the newsletter of life enrichment.

Chapter Six:
1. Arnold, Patrick M. *Wildmen, Warriors and Kings Masculine Spirituality in the Bible* (New York: Crossroad 1991) pg. 2.

Chapter Eight:
1. This is a recurring theme in Robert Moore's lectures and writings. Audio tapes of his lectures are available through the CC.G. Jung Institute of Chicago.

Chapter Nine:
1. Thompson, Keith, ed. *To be a Man in Search of the Deep Masculine* (New York: St. Martin's Press, 1991) pg. 52.
2. Ibid., pg. 39.
3. Ibid., pg. 37.
4. Ibid., pg. 43.

Chapter Ten:
1. Osherson, Samuel; *Finding Our Fathers* (New York: Ballantine Books, 1986) pg. 53.
2. Clancy, Tom; *Clear and Present Danger* (New York: G.P. Putnam's Sons, 1989) pgs. 490-492.
3. Osherson, Samuel; *Finding Our Fathers* (New York: G.P. Putnam's Sons, 1989) pgs. 54.
4. Ibid., pg. 57.

Chapter Eleven:
1. Hicks, Bob; *Uneasy Manhood* (Nashville, Tennessee: Oliver-Nelson Books, division of Thomas Nelson, Inc., 1991) pg. 45
2. Rosten, Leo; *Rosten's Treasury of Jewish Quotations* CNorthvale, New Jersey: Jason Aronson, Inc., 1988) pg. 239.
3. Walvoord, John F. and Zuck, Roy; *The BibleKnowledge Commentary* (Wheaton Illinois: Victor Books, 1985) pg 448.
4. Ibid., pg. 448.

Chapter Twelve:
1. Adapted from a sermon of Pastor John Ridler of Bethany Reformed Church, Clara City, Minnesota, December 30, 1991.

About the Author

Dr. Earl R. Henslin is a licensed marriage, family, and child therapist. His Brea, California practice through *Henslin & Associates* focuses on marriage, family, and child counseling, and he conducts training sessions and seminars for professionals such as pastors, physicians, and therapists who work in these areas. He holds the doctor of clinical psychology degree from Rosemead Graduate School of Biola University, where he is a part-time instructor. He is a member of the California Association of Marriage and Family Therapists and the Christian Association of Psychological Studies. Dr. Henslin is one the founders of Overcomers Outreach, a nonprofit ministry that assists local churches in establishing twelve-step support groups. Dr. Henslin networks closely with the Amen Clinic of Behavioral Medicine. He and his staff do assessments and evaluations for SPECT Brain Imaging Scans and follow-up care.

Henslin and Associates provides outpatient treatment and networks with different inpatient treatment facilities for the treatment of adults concerned with codependency, incest, alcoholism, drug addiction, eating disorders, sexual addiction, men's issues, and other issues of dysfunctional families. A nationally acclaimed speaker, Dr. Henslin conducts seminars on these issues for churches, Christian Organizations, counseling centers, and businesses.

For information concerning treatment programs or seminars, please contact:
Earl R. Henslin, Psy.D., M.F.C.
745 S. Brea Blvd., Suite 23
Brea, California 92821
Phone: (714) 256-2807; Fax (714) 256-0937

Other Books by Dr. Earl R. Henslin:
SECRETS OF YOUR FAMILY TREE (co-author)
FORGIVEN AND FREE:
Learn How Bible Heros with Feet of Clay Are Models for Your Recovery
YOU ARE YOUR FATHER'S DAUGHTER:
The Nurture Every Daughter Needs—The Longing When It's Lost
THE CLIFF'S EDGE:
Heaven Sent Help on a Harley—Hell Came in Other Ways